Reflections –
Beyond Thought

The Journey of a Lifetime

To Claire,
with best wishes,
Sue Sobe
13th December 13

Reflections – Beyond Thought

The Journey of a Lifetime

Susan Sosbe

BOOKS

Winchester, UK
Washington, USA

First published by O-Books, 2014
O-Books is an imprint of John Hunt Publishing Ltd., Laurel House, Station Approach,
Alresford, Hants, SO24 9JH, UK
office1@jhpbooks.net
www.johnhuntpublishing.com

For distributor details and how to order please visit the 'Ordering' section on our website.

Text copyright: Susan Sosbe 2013

ISBN: 978 1 78279 185 0

A CIP catalogue record for this book is available from the British Library.

Design: Stuart Davies

Printed and bound by CPI Group (UK) Ltd, Croydon, CR0 4YY

We operate a distinctive and ethical publishing philosophy in all
areas of our business, from our global network of authors to
production and worldwide distribution.

CONTENTS

For Katy Frances,
My Twin Soul, Teacher and Best Friend.
With Love

Acknowledgements

The writing of this book has been as much a journey as the story herein. However, it is those we meet upon the way who enrich the road we travel and it is to *all* those who have shared even the smallest part with me that I give my thanks. I also wish to thank: my daughter Katy for her love, encouragement, and belief in me and my personal goals; my friends and family for their love, support and encouragement. My deepest thanks go to Jeanette Clulow, whose qualities surpass the very meaning of the word 'friend'. Finally, I would like to thank my publisher John Hunt for giving me the opportunity to offer a profound message to many – who would otherwise be inaccessible to me.

Introduction

I sit now and smile to myself as a long awaited opportunity has finally arrived. I say opportunity perhaps inappropriately, but the chronic illness that challenged my life for so many years gifted me with an understanding of life that would help me make sense of the rest of it. My own suffering has provided not only the greatest driving force on my spiritual journey but also become my greatest teacher. Life has taught me that the only one who can change our path is the one who treads it. We may be blessed with people who love and support us, but it is for our feet to experience the terrain, alone – as willing as they may be, or as much as we may wish for them to share it.

This is a reflection of my journey and its lessons, much of which has been learnt through the guise of ill health and disability. That alone has taught me that we only learn by *living life*, rather than – *resisting it*. This book is not written for, or, directed to others with major health issues. We all have disabilities in life, both great and small. Of all the issues that have seemingly disabled me – not *all* are visible to others.

When we reflect on our lives, we look into a mirror that we may have glanced in many times before, but this time is different. We see ourselves with such clarity; almost as though a veil of dust has been shamelessly removed, revealing the purity of its own image. My journey has been a lone one but whilst no two reflections can ever be the same, I know that I am not alone in my quest to discover its truth, or indeed, to regret some of its 'mistakes'. The greatest wisdom of my journey is revealed through my acceptance of its truth but so too must I accept, without regret – the choices that led me to it. My belief that we choose, before birth, a path that will offer the perfect challenges for our spiritual advancement has perhaps eased the pain on the way.

Deep within us all is a sense of *knowing* that constantly waits in the 'wings', ready to be called. Sadly, only too often it is our *ego* that takes centre stage once more, when the power of its own deceptiveness overwhelms us all. Most of us are hesitant to believe that anything other than our *self* steers our ship, but few of us are ready to question – *who is that self?* Whilst we may be ready to accept that our unruly minds are at times in overdrive, we are reluctant to acknowledge the imposter behind the wheel. As someone who believed herself to be devoid of such an entity, this was the hardest part of the mountain to climb, as my oblivion repeatedly fed its survival. If we are truly committed to revealing our truth we must prepare ourselves to wholly experience its own nakedness, as will be revealed by the crumbling walls of our illusionary castle. The walls of illusion can only be demolished by the awakening from our dream; having once awoken, the truth of our sleeping hours becomes but a fading memory.

When we review a passage of our life in earnest, we will begin to understand and marvel at the lessons learnt and the truths revealed by some of our most challenging experiences. We will begin to question, as I have so frequently, the divine planning of some of these experiences and their role in our awakening. But perhaps for me, one of the most wondrous lessons of all is to know that enlightenment isn't a state achieved by the few, but rarely attained in a lifetime. Enlightenment is an ongoing process of exposure to truth's own illumination, the intensity of which would hurt our eyes unless we absorb it in potency, consistent with our own progress and thus, toleration of its beam. Reflection on one's life can only be experienced through the eyes of the beholder, yet in its telling – may kindle the spark of wakefulness in others on their journey. When I was a child, my father used to take me to 'Speakers' Corner' in London's Hyde Park. Those opportunities stirred something in me, as I saw myself in the most unlikely situation for a shy child – on a *Soapbox*. I spent a good part of my early life intrigued by this repeated vision, but it is only now that I understand both its meaning and the nature of my soapbox.

PART ONE

Chapter One

The surfer learns to ride the waves – not by controlling the ocean but being as One with their crest and their fall – in total mindfulness.

More than twenty-five years have elapsed since major surgery heralded the beginning of a new life for me. You could be forgiven for making assumptions about my interpretation of the word *new* and, I hasten to say, it was not the start of effortless living and dearest dreams come true. No – for me, it was an era of awakening, prompted by the hardest lessons that would be repeated over and over again, until I finally took the message to heart and remembered its teachings.

So often I hear people glibly suggesting that the so-called negative events in our lives are but lessons offered. What a wonderful thought that is; so wonderful in fact, that if I'd known it before perhaps I would be relating a very different story now. Life does have the potential to be our greatest teacher, but learning only takes place in the receptive student. Without honest and diligent heart searching, our lessons teach us nothing and we repeat them over and over again, along with our suffering. We learn no more than the nation that repeatedly believes the only way to freedom is by going to war – eventually, to annihilate itself in the process. Truth comes from our heart – not as words from our mouth.

When we seek for truth in any domain in life, the academic may well adopt a much more sophisticated approach to the rest of us in order to find it – or do they? If a doctor is attempting to diagnose his patient's condition, the common approach is by elimination. A scientist attempting to prove the efficacy of a drug or perhaps the genetic influences on certain diseases also uses sophisticated processes of elimination. These processes consist of removing, one by one, all the unwanted, superfluous data that clouds the evidence they are looking for. When we are seeking spiritual truth – don't we need to use a similar process? It all seems so familiar doesn't it, but if we continue to take our enquiry solely on the path of the scientist, we may never be satisfied with our findings. So what is different about the scientist and the spiritual seeker? Indeed, the scientist may be a spiritual seeker and he may apply the same scientific method-ology to his enquiry, but the one thing he may not consider is whether he looks for truth or proof. There are many ways of proving a theory or hypothesis and that proof will also constitute its truth (which will satisfy the scientist), but as hard as we try, we will never prove spiritual truth. We can wire people up to elaborate equipment and record all sorts of data whilst perhaps they receive healing; experience psychic phenomena; enter a meditative state and so forth. We may be able to persuade a doctor or scientist to substantiate the effects of any kind of 'energy healing' on the human body; these changes having been observed and documented in various parts of the world using technical imagery. As a healer, I know only too well how satis-fying it is when a person's recovery from a life-threatening cancer has been attributed to healing. I also know the doubt that lurks in the minds of some without the relevant proof. It's true that the disappearance of a cancer (or any other disease) concurrent with healing doesn't prove anything, but doesn't the disappearance of this cancer demonstrate the natural ability of our body to heal itself – unless, of course, it was wrongly diagnosed in the first place? Shouldn't the beauty of our physical encasement and its absolute perfection of design be at the very core of our enquiry? The more earnestly we seek, the more effec-tively we eliminate the unwanted data that clouds our path, until we finally unveil something that only its beholder can recognize – our *Truth*.

Chapter Two

Seeking spiritual truth and trying to make sense of life and the world therein has been an ongoing enquiry for me as long as I can remember. Even as a young child I knew there was more to life than that which I witnessed around me; our progression to a life beyond the physical body was a natural acceptance. A painful shyness for much of my early childhood progressed to a lack of confidence until I was out of my teens, but I realize now that what was probably seen as a lack of self-esteem couldn't have been further from the truth. I wonder now how many other youngsters are wearing the wrong label. Although I came from a loving yet somewhat dysfunctional family with all its problems, I always felt as though I was on the outside looking in. Discovering the truth about my childlike expectations 'that everyone experienced life as I did' – was probably the major cause of both my shyness and my lack of confidence. Strangely though, I was still driven by an inner *knowing* that would remain silent, until the time was right. Even as my heart ached when I sensed the energy of sickness, distress, or discord around me, my hands would reach out to heal; expressing, what only much later I knew to be, my gift. Reflection on these early days reveals to me that 'the young shy girl' was not in fact one who was too nervous to speak, but one who was fast understanding that few people spoke her language. The only way I knew how to communicate my truth was through touch – healing touch. Somehow, from the age of around four or five years, my hands were naturally drawn to making people feel better, as my late father would remember.

Why do people so frequently ridicule the men who are unfortunate enough to lose their hair? I have never been able to understand this unkindness any more than I could understand why my father (who began losing his hair at a very early age) went along with the humour of it. I knew my dad suffered greatly at losing his crowning glory that was the envy of any female in his youth. And yet, no one seemed to appreciate his bereavement, apart from his Victorian mother who, in his childhood, dressed him in suitable velvet attire to complement his luxurious locks for the benefit of the camera. No wonder Dad became so camera shy in adulthood, despite his good looks and gleaming smile. I don't think my grandmother so much understood his loss as much as she indulged in her own sadness. My father had many of his own issues to deal with, and the disquiet and mental torment of his mind was something that, sadly, would not be healed in this life. I could, however, put my hands on his head and at the same time as helping his hair to grow allow his soul to soak up the healing energy. I loved my father dearly, and as the years went on never gave up desperately wanting to find that place of peace and healing for him. But whilst his bald patch responded by producing downy new growth, his mind became increasingly troubled and he was too frightened to acknowledge (until I was an adult) what really was being given through the channel of my hands.

'Could do better – spends much of the math lesson daydreaming!' Little did they know – I was far from daydreaming, but I did spend much of my time in a different place, another 'world'. The realization that the entire class was waiting anxiously for some sort of response from me caught me out time and time again. My body was so shocked when I was inconsiderately brought back to earth that I used to tremble inside, having absolutely no idea what was expected of me let alone what lesson I was in. French was another favourite lesson to remove myself from, although I was rarely able to stay away uninterrupted! The French teacher had a booming voice and seemed to believe the best way to teach the 'slow ones' was by towering over them with her voluptuous bosom and terrifying them into learning the unfamiliar language. How I wish now that I had saved my 'away days' for another lesson; but also, how I regret not learning until very recently what a very gentle soul she actually was. My only experience of her more gentle side was when she stopped halfway through a lesson, not to ridicule me in front of the class for my 'absence', but to comment on the brilliance of my school blouse! She asked me what soap powder my mother used but I was too surprised to tell her that actually – I was in charge of the family laundering and I used whatever was on special offer.

My inability to be wholly present on this plane has been an ongoing difficulty for me throughout my life and even as I write these words, I revel in the nature of my creativity which, as with all creativity, lies far beyond the tapping fingers and the thinking mind. *Running home* when things get too difficult to handle always seems an easy option. For me, like the young teenager who runs back to mum when things don't work out, *home* was and still remains a place of safety and quiet serenity – a place where I don't have to explain or work out – a place just to be.

Chapter Three

When I was told that much of my stomach had been removed as a matter of necessity, I was both shocked and relieved. Only the previous day, I had given my friend a nightmare three hour drive across country from the South Coast to Oxford (where we both lived) with a leaking petrol tank and excruciating abdominal pain. We stopped on the motorway every few miles whilst I was handed a plastic bag and waited for the searing pain to relent, until the next wave. The constant possibility of being escorted off the hard shoulder and into the nearest hospital by the police was one concern too many. I had 'agreed' with my friend that – my condition had only taken hold since we were on the motorway. I was, of course, oblivious to the leaking tank! My inability to lie was thankfully not put to the test.

Apart from the miracle of getting to Oxford safely and the second one of surviving the physical onslaught to my body, I experienced another that only I can substantiate. Before leaving my parents' home I had been in continuous, unrelenting agony and yet, I knew that I must return to Oxford. As did everyone around me, I prayed for the physical strength to get us there safely. I became totally focused from the beginning of the journey, reluctant to even answer the concerned enquiries from Susan as to how I was doing. It seemed as though I had stepped beyond what my mind was telling me and entered a place of peace that I could only describe as a surreal analgesia. It was a crazy thing to do, madness that I still question. I should have allowed my family to call the ambulance and headed for the nearest hospital but for some reason, I knew if I did I would probably be telling my story through a spiritual medium right now.

I was surprised things had become so bad for me since I was just looking forward to going back to work after another period of sick leave. It seemed that at long last (after many months of pain and anguish), the doctors were finally making progress with a diagnosis and I was anticipating my next appointment with greater optimism. I had spent the last eighteen months sitting, fortnightly, in the outpatients department of the hospital where I was a nurse teacher. Interspersed with these appointments I underwent many tests of varying unpleasantness and medication, including antidepressants – the only help seemingly offered for many undiagnosed conditions. During the next few years, I would discover how readily doctors reach for such drugs rather than accepting and admitting that they just don't know. Far from destroying my faith in medicine, such an admission would have restored my own personal power in exchange for the *patient label* I had now been awarded and had finally come to accept.

So now it was over. My car had been dispatched to the garage and I was dispatched to hospital, although not before insisting on washing my hair and having a bath! It seemed that I had some sort of notion that washing my hair would make me feel better, or maybe I just wanted to pass to the next life respectably prepared. My oblivion to the seriousness and urgency of the situation frustrated my friend considerably. I don't think I was really oblivious to the facts but more likely, didn't have the strength to fight any more. As I lay on the trolley in the emergency room I believed the agonizing pain itself would take me, let alone the cause of the pain. I needed some powerful persuasion to give my consent to surgery, which was evidently now a matter of dire need.

Chapter Four

I had managed to survive the threat to my life; what a relief. My health issues of the previous months had erupted like that of a smouldering volcano. All I had to do now was see myself fit and well and back to work in a few weeks or so. What else would I expect after such an ordeal and knowing that the offending part of my anatomy had now been removed? But this was just the start of a new and very long voyage.

Life was quite exciting and certainly eventful in the next twenty years or so, demonstrating a degree of synchronicity that has always intrigued and convinced me that there *is* a 'greater plan'. In October of the same year as my gastrectomy I became engaged and later married to a man I had met exactly one year prior to my surgery. I had felt so indignant when my manager told me I had either to take, or lose, the leave due to me at the end of the financial year. There were always difficulties squeezing in leave between teaching blocks but I had worked so hard that I certainly wasn't going to forfeit it again, so I made a last minute arrangement to visit Athens. It was so last minute that I had to urge the travel agent to persevere in finding me the only remaining booking! Three days later, at the start of Easter, I was heading for the Athenian splendour. On the same trip as me were two delightful people who were meeting up with a close friend they'd worked with in the Middle East. He was apparently on a business trip which coincided with their holiday, making it a perfect opportunity for a reunion. After sharing a long and arduous day sightseeing, Ken and Mary had insisted on me joining them all, which I politely refused on the grounds of tiredness. Actually, I couldn't imagine their poor friend wanting to share their precious reunion with an intruder he had never met, but my ardent refusal was in vain and as a result I was almost tricked into joining them. Sheepishly approaching the hotel lounge, I saw the back of a man with my two new friends sitting either side of him. Knowing that I hadn't been seen, I swiftly turned around away from their table, but strangely, almost by magic, their friend turned round and looked at me, attracting the attention of Ken and Mary who by this time were eagerly beckoning me to my seat. I am often in wonderment when I consider the role of fate or design in my life to date, and question regularly the map I seem to be following. How many people's lives would have been quite different had fate not pushed its hand in some way or other? We will never know, but we can begin to acknowledge the role such synchronicity has played in our lives.

After our marriage, Richard had to return to the Middle East alone because I was still not fit enough to join him. We had spent our honeymoon in beautiful Tuscany, with me still only able to take less than baby portions of food due to my newly plumbed anatomy. I then spent another three months in hospital having more surgery and treatment before we could finally celebrate our union together, yet again – exactly one year after my first surgery. Easter time has its own remembrance for me, which makes it a doubly significant time in my life.

In the long days without Richard, my second stay in hospital was immensely difficult. Apart from the pain I was in, I was suffering in other ways. It was hard to believe that I was now married, with a home I hadn't even seen in Kuwait and a husband I had seen for only ten days at Christmas since our wedding in October. Richard had his own mourning and his own issues before we were married, and our separation stirred feelings in me far beyond my own personal needs in our relationship. I was enveloped in guilt as I sensed his sadness and loneliness whilst his suffering became my suffering. However hard I tried and however much I reasoned my own inability to prevent what was happening, I couldn't eradicate my feelings of guilt for unwittingly messing up Richard's new life as well as my own. As I struggled with my emotions within the confines of the hospital walls, nothing could have prepared me for the way I would one day express them.

Lying on my bed, having had a call from my husband in Kuwait the previous evening, I don't remember having any particular thoughts other than those that frequently occupied my mind. I constantly worried about the predictable effects of my health on our relationship if I didn't get better. I had no reason at all to feel that Richard would love me any the less, but my own expectations of renewed health were fast disappearing and the guilt grew with my fear. On reflection, I suspect that a substantial part of my emotions was compounded by the institutionalisation within the relative safety of the hospital ward. My excitement for travel and my new life was waning, together with my energy, as I began to believe both my marriage and the history of our relationship was in fact a dream.

I looked up from the book I was reading. Quite unexpectedly, like a mirage in the desert, I saw Richard walking towards me holding a bouquet of flowers and beaming all over his face. But this was no mirage or illusion. I was hit like a thunderbolt with an array of emotions which were so alien to me I had no idea how to deal with them. I was of course thrilled to see him – once I had got my head round the fact that he was in London, when he should have been in Kuwait. I was confused and at the same time angry. What a lovely thing for him to have done to surprise me like that and yet, he had unwittingly invaded my personal space, my thoughts, my reactions, all without warning. Most painful of all was to *know* the hurt I had caused the person I loved so much as a result of my own apparent momentary rejection of him. Even as I write these words I still feel the pain of that place; as deeply as I search, will never quite understand what happened to me, in that brief moment. Little did I know that our heart wrenching goodbyes after our short reunion would be the last before I finally went back with Richard to Kuwait, just one month later and yes – yet again, just past Easter and my birthday, in the month of April. Still quite seriously debilitated, I had managed to persuade both the medics and Richard that I was ready to leap, or more accurately – fly! This was the time for me to face my fears of the unknown, but with the love and support of my dear husband. Nothing would persuade me to wait any longer.

Chapter Five

The drive from the airport into Safat (in Kuwait) was like a dream that I constantly thought I'd wake up from. Numerous cars were just abandoned on the highway almost in memory of the accidents that had rendered them worthless. Life suddenly seemed cheap and cars, even cheaper. How intriguing, that I was later to witness such apparent poverty in a country that was so wealthy and, indeed, one I should come to have great affection for.

Our driver, a lovely Indian man called Govendan, proudly stopped the car outside our apartment as though he was personally responsible for choosing it for us. I suspect that was largely the truth. As the car door was opened I was almost thrown back with the smell of drains and the heat, which was like walking into a raging furnace. I found it all so surreal that I couldn't take it in, but I was home at last and could now start living again. We were about to start a very long honeymoon – until death would us part.

Our stay in Kuwait was relatively brief but long enough for the healing process, which seemed part of my destiny, to take effect on both a physical and spiritual level. Because we didn't live in the ex-pat community and due to the restrictions placed upon my gender, I spent many hours on my own in the apartment just looking at the sea in front of me. I have never felt so at peace and far removed from any of my perpetual worries in life. I believe now that (as difficult as it was to leave them) those two years away from family and all my concerns were instrumental in building the solid foundations of our relationship.

By the end of our first year, finally beginning to feel recovered and back to my old self, I became desperate to have a baby. I say desperate because those were the feelings that suddenly came over me and although we both hoped that one day we would have a child, it certainly hadn't been considered high on the agenda. I didn't know quite how I would put it to Richard and when I did, true to his style – I wished for an hour or so that I hadn't. Again, quite predictably, he'd taken his thoughts away with him and come back concerned, but as enthusiastic as me. All that was needed was for me to get pregnant; a seemingly unlikely event in my circumstances, combined with the fact that I only had one patent fallopian tube! Richard was understandably worried about my health, but I knew from the depths of my *being* that it was now or never. It had to be now and I would somehow be alright.

About six weeks pregnant (having conceived in the Nile Valley), any uncertainties I may have had about Richard's feelings about an addition to the family were completely negated. He had only just arrived at his office. On hearing the news, he did no more than return home in a state of childlike excitement to be shown the evidence of the positive testing kit! By the end of the week he had, unbelievably, told just about everyone. I wonder yet again at the timing of our daughter's conception, which took place during our visit to a country that my soul had literally yearned to take me. Richard came home one evening and put an envelope down on the table, asking me to open it. I remember it so well. The solemn look on his face made my heart pound somewhat, but I should by then have known something of his wry sense of humour. As I opened the envelope I could hardly control my emotions. I was holding tickets for a week in Cairo, followed by a trip up the Nile to Luxor and Aswan. How I would survive the heat and the early morning starts I didn't know, but I did know that this trip was part of my spiritual journey.

When we arrived at Cairo Airport we had the great honour of being met and escorted out by Kamahl, the ex-chief of police. I don't know what we'd have done without this wonderful man because the throng of people all trying to find their way to *somewhere* was literally breathtaking! Richard was clearly getting anxious about my inability to stay upright as I was unwillingly jostled this way and that against my will or indeed better judgment. Just as I was wondering if we would ever reach passport control, let alone retrieve our cases, we were greeted with the smiling face of Kamahl before being swiftly and purposefully marched, not to the front of the queue, but straight to passport control! Who did make these amazing arrangements for us, I wondered? I will never really know but it was just one of many kindnesses that I experienced throughout my time in the Middle East. On one occasion, Kamahl took this kindness way past the call of duty (even for an ex-chief of police) when he became frustrated by the traffic jam caused by a lane closure; not really unusual for Cairo. Kamahl quickly directed his driver, as he got out of the car himself, removed the metal barrier and ushered our car through! I was never completely sure if that was a gesture of consideration for us or, indeed, the extent of his intolerance of being kept waiting but nevertheless, another memorable occasion within my own memory bank.

Perhaps the greatest lesson for us to learn on our spiritual journey is to overcome doubt and trust our *inner knowing* that is so often enshrouded by our own thoughts. It was a difficult time for me when I first discovered that my energy had suddenly been so sapped from my body again, making me dependent on Richard for everything. The independent, self-sufficient person who always struggled to be in control was, it seemed, being tested yet again, when finally I was forced to accept help. Had I learnt nothing from the pain I had already endured? What part of me was constantly resisting? It would be considerably further down my path before I would find out. As if I wasn't being challenged enough, I went to the bathroom one day with abdominal cramps, only to have my worst fears confirmed. Every day for the next eight weeks, I expected to lose our most precious gift.

But I was going to keep our baby because I knew – I had to. Babies abort quite naturally and seemingly easily in the first trimester of pregnancy. I have sat holding the hand of many a mother, comforting her after she lost the baby growing inside her. Apart from Richard (who never knew how critical things were), nobody tried to allay my fears. No tests or investigations were done to establish what was going on inside my womb and yet I had the highest respect for the medical team. Such was the philosophy both of the medics and, it seemed, the mothers-to-be, that the foetus who wants to abort knows best and should be allowed to do so without intervention. I was being brutally challenged now by something I too had always believed, whilst I earnestly tried to put my trust in the place from whence came that belief.

As I battled fortnightly through a sea of excitable and impatient Arab women to reach the door of the obstetrician's consulting room, I mentally checked my decision to have my baby in the State Hospital rather than the private one expected of me. As I write these words, I realize how enriched my life has been through this experience and never for a minute regret my decision, confusing and somewhat frightening though it may have been at times.

Our baby, unperturbed by the challenges already on offer, finally settled quietly (or otherwise) into her safe haven for the remaining six months. Perhaps it was just too comfortable for her in there and I'd wondered at times whether she had changed her mind! Richard was constantly anxious about the 'labour run' and whether he would manage to get me to the hospital on time. It was rather different to the predictable routine that most pregnant mothers can anticipate in Britain.

He needn't have worried. Fate took the concerns away from him, only to give him other things to think about. After one of my antenatal consultations it was decided that a small heart problem I had was best dealt with in hospital, just one week before I was due to give birth. It was a shock to both of us being prematurely parted for reasons we least expected. But *shock* didn't come into it as Richard escorted me through the doors of Sabbha Hospital. And that was as far as he was allowed to come with me. I didn't speak Arabic and didn't even have a chance to say goodbye as I was led through one door and he through the other, almost like the 'Ladies' and 'Gents'. So much was happening and it felt unreal. I suddenly realized that I had absolutely no idea what to expect as this woman, clad in Islamic dress, rushed me through corridors, lifts, and wards. All I could gather, as I now became quite anxious, was that no one had wanted me, let alone been prepared for their new admission. At last we found a ward that could accommodate me, or so I thought. I was led down a large open ward that certainly lacked the sort of clinical feel I was used to in a hospital, but neither did it have the feel of 'home' that so many midwives now strive to provide for their mothers. It seemed all so informal, and at the same time uninformed – certainly about me anyway. As we walked through the ward, apparently hoping to find me an empty bed, the occasional sleepy Arab woman glared disapprovingly as we disturbed her afternoon nap. I began to feel quite out of place as I realized I was the only European in the hospital. The nurse who accompanied me (at least I think she was a nurse) approached a bed that lacked the crisp white clean linen I was used to, gestured for me to take up occupancy, then went away. I hesitantly got in, though not before examining the positive grubbiness of all the beds around me, but this one was (not surprisingly) uninviting. No sooner had I plucked up the courage to get between the sheets had I jumped out again, the rightful resident screaming at me from the trolley on which she was being wheeled into the ward. So off I went again, not knowing whether to laugh or cry, in search of a comfortable bed to rest my weary self and try to discover where my husband was. This was a truly, truly surreal experience, and at the time not one that I was enjoying. I contemplated running out but had the awful feeling I might find the doors were locked and besides – where would I go and how would I get home?

I was found another bed, but this time by someone I identified quite definitely as a nurse. Her dress was not dissimilar to our own nurses' uniforms, but even more important for me was that she spoke some English. Perhaps it is too presumptuous of me to believe it was only our verbal communication that eased my anxiety because I know this to be untrue. This woman was dressed familiarly, spoke familiarly and yes – was of a nationality (Indian) that was very familiar to me in my own country and my own profession. As one who believes no boundaries should separate us, I am urged to ask myself, what judgments might have been going on in my own mind and from whence did those judgments come? By choice I had ended up having my baby in completely unfamiliar surroundings with a language barrier that seemingly thwarted all my attempts to communicate effectively. The experience was one that I had chosen and it was up to me to discover its teachings, together with all the other lessons life offers me.

I didn't have to think about Richard's disappearance any more. The ward doors opened and in came a throng of people from all directions clearly set for a party. It was really exciting and again a display that I could never have contemplated when I was a Ward Sister – liberal though I may have been. I didn't really understand what was happening to begin with and didn't know how I would tolerate the noise *or* lack of privacy if it was a regular occurrence. The chaps had entered the ward like porters, each carrying at least two cases of soda on their shoulders and I was the first to be thrown a couple of cans; no communication barrier there! Richard came in and explained that it was all part of the weekend celebration, hence the length of visiting that day. Friday was the Holy day when the men went to the mosque for prayers and everyone was away from work. Sunday afternoon was also free.

As I saw Richard looking for me, I was overwhelmed with a reality of my hospitalization that I hadn't even thought about. Filled with so many emotions, I was dying to be in his arms to comfort him and for him to comfort me, but the realization that we couldn't even hold hands for however long it took our baby to enter the world was unbearable. Both of us pretended it wasn't happening and made desperate attempts to stay strong for the other. As I looked around, I saw fathers barely glancing at the beautiful new addition to their family in the crib beside their wife's bed, let alone demonstrate any kind of affection towards her. He couldn't of course because it was unlawful to do so and unless I wanted to have my baby in prison, we too would need to respect the laws of Kuwait – of Islam. But now, we were sharing a cell in our own prison. I couldn't help but wonder what the topics of conversation between couples were, and whether their worries and aspirations for their children would be similar to those we might have later. It was like being in another world even though I had been in Kuwait for almost two years now, but the love and affection that surrounded us by the friends and employees of Richard (numbering no less than sixteen nationalities) was something worth coming for. I had no idea that the love and friendship that had already touched my heart would be repeated in Sabbha Hospital when I discovered there truly are no boundaries to love – except that of our own making.

I was quickly known as 'the heart case' by the nurses (which was a bit off-putting) and it was decided to give me a bed in a quieter room. To my amazement and distress, my roommate turned out to be an elderly lady who was all of eighty years and clearly suffering; probably preparing to leave this world. 'What was she doing on this ward?' – I thought. I had seen several women about who most definitely were not mothers-to-be. The poor old lady moaned and groaned, and eventually I took the courage to sit with her and hold her hand. She looked at me with her toothless smile and, yet again, my memory was imprinted with an experience I will never forget.

I walked out into the main ward to stretch my legs. One nurse was pushing a trolley laden with packets of disposable diapers, as the multimillion-dollar international nappy company took the opportunity to imprint their name on the new mother's memory. She deposited them at the end of each bed whilst another followed her with bottles of milk, which were delivered in a more unconventional way as the mothers raised their arms and prepared to catch. No strong views on breastfeeding here!

I had now been in hospital for almost a week but still hadn't given birth. It seemed that I was becoming a 'long stayer', as I observed with envy the quick turnover of other mothers. No sooner had I devised a method of communication with a face that I recognized, than they went – to their homes I assumed. But there was to be a surprise for me. I was told that I was moving yet again to another place, but wasn't given any details. It took me a while to work out how it had all happened. No longer would Richard and I have to behave as though there was an invisible wall between us. With the help of his company's Kuwaiti partner, he had found me a private room that I'd not even realized was available. By visiting time, I was quite ecstatic.

Visiting time became party time for Richard. My tea arrived, together with a big slab of ultra-sweet cake that could have fed four people. The cake delivery was a daily occurrence but so too was a tin of sterilized cream with my breakfast and two eggs! The eggs were at least appealing to me, until I sedately cracked the shell on the bed table and found myself bathed in dripping raw yolk. I never did find out how I was intended to eat them but the only weight issues that this mother in waiting had was one of emaciation. This wasn't the case for the Egyptian ladies who befriended me. No wonder they shared such disbelief that I wasn't even pregnant, yet alone already overdue. They looked at me, sizing me up, until I began to wonder myself if I really was having a baby and, once again, if we were all part of some elaborate dream. But these ladies were all large – very large. Most of them unsurprisingly were diabetic, which increasingly interested me as I considered the effects on their unborn babies. I reflected frequently on the diet I was offered daily. The sweet tooth had taken over in the Middle Eastern culture and the price was seemingly being paid.

My waters had broken – something of a surprise to me. Where was my mind, I wondered, before remembering why I was in hospital? I recall the feeling of excitement combined with that of sudden fear. I was totally unprepared for what to expect and suddenly realized that I hadn't even discussed it with anyone let alone attended anything remotely like antenatal classes. I was whisked off to the labour ward where the piercing sounds of that more like the distress calls of female hyenas assaulted my senses. I was no longer a confident, caring nurse but just another very frightened woman who had no idea what was happening to her or her unborn child.

Ten, fifteen, twenty hours went by as I peered sleepily at the clock on the wall. Constantly being jabbed with needles, presumably giving me pain relief and thus sedation. I was left wondering what the effect was on my infant, but there was nobody around who seemed to make sense of my incoherent enquiry. Quite clearly there was a job to be done and I seemed a very unimportant part of that task as far as asking questions was concerned. I hadn't seen my husband or had contact with him since I told him I was in labour the day before. The only men around were doctors, and women were coming and going on trolleys like a conveyor belt. Maybe it was a good idea that I was all but 'knocked out'.

But not for much longer; Katy Frances had decided to leave her place of solitude and join us at last. No one ever told me of the emotions I would feel as I held her in my arms, but maybe they were for me alone? How would anyone know what I experience, and why would I expect you to perceive the expression of those feelings? Can any of us really do that? As I reached out in gratitude for the hand of the doctor who had delivered our daughter, she was clearly both awkward and confused by my emotions; as though my reaction was something she hadn't witnessed before. Was I really different or perhaps it was the drugs or hormone changes? Why was my reaction to the birth of my daughter different to any of the other women visiting the labour ward? Were my cultural differences the most significant clue to the answers I wanted, and if so, what made it so? At what point does nature emerge through nurture I wonder, and what holds us back? These were my questions but the answers would be a long time coming.

I couldn't wait to see Richard but was told that I needed the rest and wouldn't be out of the delivery unit until after visiting time. This meant I wouldn't see him for another twenty-four hours! Now what new mother and baby could bear that? An hour later, we were on our way back to my own little room with a very, very, proud father following through the doors shortly after us. Within twenty-four hours, being surrounded by a sea of beaming faces, we knew that we were not the only ones celebrating Katy's arrival. There was hardly room for me as our friends of all nationalities came to express their joy of the occasion. The inability to speak each other's language was of little significance; the love and joy that surrounded us spoke profoundly and truthfully – from the heart, but not the lips. *This*, I thought, 'is why I came here – to this hospital – to this country, and what better greetings into this world could you have, Katy Frances?' Others showed their joy in a different way. My dear father raised his glass of medicinal brandy from his own hospital bed, before quietly closing his eyes for the last time. Clearly knowing that we were both safe and well, he could finally walk free of both his lifelong mental imprisonment and the cancer that he, until now, sadly but bravely fought to deny. Strangely too, before his diagnosis when I was four months pregnant, I kissed him goodbye before returning to Kuwait, knowing it would be the last kiss I would give him. My dad passed on to greener pastures, without me even being there.

Four months later and our time in the Middle East had come to an end. Richard had been made an offer he couldn't refuse, back in the UK office. As excited as we were, I knew we would both suffer some culture shock on our return, but I was more than aware that my two years in Kuwait was a holiday break compared to the many years that Richard had lived in various parts of the Middle East. The departure lounge was seemingly full of our many friends and colleagues coming to see us off, in true Middle Eastern style. With tears filling our eyes with emotion, we waved goodbye for the last time before passing through passport control. But as our friends headed home, perhaps mentally anticipating our progress as they travelled, few would have expected the chaos our baby was now causing. Richard, being the male of the family, naturally passed through passport control first! His residence permit was cancelled and he was beaming on the other side of the gate awaiting Katy and me (she was on my passport) to come through. But as though her entrance into the world had not been dramatic enough for her, it was announced that she didn't have an exit visa and couldn't go through to the awaiting plane! At first, I wondered if it were all a joke or something but quickly realized that it wasn't; experience should have told me not to have such expectations. So Richard was one side of the barrier, unable to come back in and I was on the other side, unable to pass through because I had a four month old baby who didn't have permission to leave. We showed them her birth certificate both in Arabic and that issued by the British Consulate, but to no avail. Now becoming decidedly anxious as I listened to the excited and somewhat irate voices of both my husband and the immigration officers, I knew that the British Airways plane would soon have to leave without us. The strength of Richard's voice, now indicating his own frustrations and anger, made me thankful that he was indeed on the other side of the barrier; there was more than enough to worry about. Quite suddenly, there was a change in facial expressions and a quietening of voices. Richard indicated to me not to worry as he disappeared through a door and by the time I was truly saying my prayers, he had emerged with a grin on his face that stretched from ear to ear. There were handshakes all round. The gates were opened for us and Richard sped down the corridor with Katy in his arms to the awaiting plane, which had now been delayed for over half an hour. The applause as we entered the cabin was something I will never forget and, as I strapped myself in, remembered that I hadn't asked what magic had suddenly befallen upon us. It transpired that our guardian angel was no more than the company's Kuwaiti partner again; the same man who, only the week before, had tried to persuade Richard to stay in Kuwait with the added temptation of a job for me too! How fortuitous that he was still in residence. Just a phone call away and there was another person and another kindness to remember.

Chapter Six

When living in another country, most of us at some time yearn for the familiarity of our homeland, regardless of our enjoyment of the experience. Whilst living in the Middle East, that yearning for me related to the absence of green pastures and, furthermore, the restrictions imposed upon my gender. For many expatriates, the constant personal yearning sadly jeopardizes a unique opportunity to experience themselves in another environment. Such is their resistance to all that is unfamiliar; they effectively safeguard their comfort zone by selectively seeking the company of their own kind. It's interesting to observe how differently we select our comrades when we're away from home. We become far less discriminating about the people we choose to fraternize with, even a common language satisfying our needs. It is this nostalgia for home territory that reflects our feelings of anxiety, uncertainty and *not belonging,* but it is our resistance to what is that prevents us from experiencing its truth – resulting in further disharmony between us and our environment. So, very sadly, many discard the most precious gifts of their journey in favour of their overriding need to feel safe in familiarity; unfortunately, that place becomes so safe that the journey becomes one of little adventure and therefore limited growth. When we make a financial investment, the return we receive is appropriate to the element of risk we take. We cannot expect to become rich when we are not prepared for a bit of discomfort on the way, but if we just want somewhere to keep our money safe without growth – we don't invest it at all.

'If only I knew then what I know now.' How many of us have uttered these words during our life? All knowledge seems simplistic at the time we experience and understand it; the knowledge we gain today was our mystery of yesterday, so we need to be open to what we may not know today but will do tomorrow. That can be a daunting and yet exciting thought for us. So often, when we look back, we realize that if we'd been presented with all the knowledge we have now, we would have been completely overwhelmed by it.

It's with regret that we so often recognize our 'mistakes' of yesterday, in the belief that we have somehow lost valuable time. We don't necessarily make the best choices in life and, even when we do, the nature of life means that we get bitten occasionally, regardless of our efforts. But it's not time that we've lost but the wonderful opportunity contained within that time, when we regret rather than value the lessons within it. When we allow ourselves to consciously live every moment and every experience, regret becomes a language of the past. When I look back on my days in the Middle East I can have no regrets, except that of my fear caused by a lack of understanding of another culture and its people, people I had previously judged – in accordance to what I perceived as our differences. How wrong I would have been and how grateful I am to have had the window of opportunity that let me experience my own truth, in theirs. When I look back, I see that this was a very special time in my life but I also view it as another chapter that has now ended. As with the chapters in any book, by its very nature each will tell its own story, but standing alone without the chapters that precede or follow – its meaning is lost. As the one experiencing the book through its text, rarely can the ending be determined by the beginning. Any chapter at any time can change the outcome unexpectedly and dramatically, reminding us to value both that which we perceive as the *good* and the *bad* experiences in life. What seemed bad yesterday may reveal its benefits tomorrow and vice versa. Tempting though it is, we cannot truly judge any experience as good or bad since the purpose of our existence is to grow spiritually and, whether we know it at the time or not – life will always offer us the food to feed that growth.

There are many chapters to our lives of course and some are much shorter than others. Maybe, due to their unpleasant nature, we may be relieved to see these short periods flash past and will often try to forget them as best we can. Quite the reverse happens, not infrequently, when the short episodes may seemingly feel so good that we try desperately to hold on to them and their memories; our lives tending to seesaw repeatedly up and down, but we never seem to get the balance quite right. Although some people struggle more than others to find that balance, let alone maintain it, many of us spend much of our lives hoping for better days to come and, when they arrive, spend those precious moments fearfully anticipating their reversal. It's probably more accurate to say that, rather than consciously trying to maintain a balance in our lives, we search for more of what we perceive as *good* experiences. When we learn to accept and welcome *all* our experiences whilst being completely *present* in them all, we dissolve the pain of the 'bad' and heighten the joy of the 'good', knowing that neither is part of us anyway. We don't and can't hold on to any experience and, in that knowledge, we will maintain perfect balance all the time, but we seem to find that so difficult to achieve. Sometimes such bad things happen to us that our lives are changed instantly, never to be the same again. But for some, even after horrific ordeals, emerges an ability to transcend the pain and heal the soul by transforming their own suffering into something positive. Time and time again, society is indebted to these people who have humbly dedicated the rest of their own lives to preventing the suffering of others, by exploiting the wisdom of their own pain.

Chapter Seven

My body weak, tired and painful, I used to reflect on the way my family and I should have enjoyed each other. That was before my husband gently but firmly reminded me of what we did have and what we did share together, rather than what we were missing. I needed those words to be repeated more than once, but if my writing could offer nothing else or I could give a gift to the world, his words would be the gift I would choose. Whenever I feel life isn't going to plan – my plan, I hear his words resounding in my head.

Chronic illness doesn't just arrive one day like an appendicitis or influenza, when one minute it strikes you down but by the time you notice its inconvenience, it's gone. It seems to sneak in unsuspectingly like an uninvited guest that's lost its way, taking the wrong path into your physical domain. Thence on it seems, our visitor feels so at home that it completely forgets just who the guest is and begins to dominate the entire scene. Chronic illness isn't a disease entity in itself and the doctor doesn't say that you are suffering from 'chronic illness' because, more often than not, he or she isn't privy to that information any more than you are. Chronic does no more than describe the course of events, but sadly, it is frequently only after the numerous tests and investigations mingled with bad days, better days and deterioration that a pattern begins to emerge; a pattern that lasts for weeks, months and then years. Every test and every investigation, however unpleasant, brings new hope and optimism. Every day that is mysteriously better than the one before, or even the long awaited remission, lulls you into false security. A diagnosis or even a cure are the all-pervading thoughts and prayers you have every hospital visit as your mind, unwilling to let you down, takes control with the perpetual dialogue with itself. All the alarm bells are ringing, but you don't hear – yet.

I know all about tests, investigations and hospitalization. I know all about false hope and the despair that comes from receiving a new diagnosis just as you are coming to terms with the last one, or much worse, not receiving one at all. I know what it's like to discover you've received the wrong treatment for the wrong diagnosis for fourteen years. I know what it's like to feel the frustration, finally accepting that your body is no longer able to function as it did; to have hardly enough energy to sit at the table and put food into your mouth, let alone cook it. I know what it's like to be in continuous unrelenting pain right through your body. I know what it's like to wonder if anyone can truly under-stand what I feel. I know what it's like to discover – this is my journey, my lessons and my choice – to use a disability as a beautiful gift by which to grow or an ugly burden to suffer.

Observations on my spiritual journey have taught me that there is no difference between a chronic health problem and any other kind of chronic problem we have in life. They are both life situa-tions from which we cannot just escape, but challenges that we all face. No sooner are there signs of things getting better than we are cruelly thrown into the abyss once more. The curious thing about this chain of events is that it keeps repeating itself over and over again, until we discover and address the reasons for that repetition.

It has become my belief that these recurrent issues we face in life are indeed lessons upon the way and the repetition does come to an end, once we realize that. No good teacher will just give up on a child who clearly doesn't understand the essence of what he is being taught. How fruitless it would be if we introduced the teaching of a new subject by starting at the top, when there was no foundation on which to build further knowledge. Life is a journey, for which we all have a map. Although we may all start off in the south and be heading for Scotland, we soon discover there are many varying routes to our destination, but the one destined for each of us is influenced by both the knowledge we already have and the experience we need to further that knowledge. The more times we make a journey, the more experienced we become in recognizing the terrain and choosing the best route for us. We must remember that whilst some will like the scenic route, others prefer the speed of the motorway. What seemed the highest level of difficulty before soon becomes a stroll in the park.

However humble we are, most of us seek what we commonly call 'success'. However, our perception of this word will vary widely, some even believing it to be quite inappropriate for a book that seeks to explore our spiritual nature. For many of us, the word just screams out financial wealth, high living, exotic holidays, examinations passed and so forth. And for some, any one of these attainments is indeed acknowledgement of our achievement upon which we will probably build further. So does this mean that the student who leaves school without furthering his education is unsuccessful? If this word has so many meanings to us all, maybe it's one that should be excluded from our vocabulary lest, yet again, we make dangerous judgments based on our own belief system. But rather than dismiss words that we all seem to interpret differently, maybe we should seek to understand the real meaning? The Oxford Dictionary says that 'success' is – the achievement of a goal or purpose. We will have many goals in our lives and hopefully many achievements but our lives have only *one* purpose and to achieve that is surely a time to celebrate our success.

Chapter Eight

I hadn't appreciated what an undemanding, quiet life I was living in Kuwait. Even with our entertaining commitments, the leisurely existence of my day was something that might be envied by my busy friends back home. It was a strange experience at first since I'd always been, least politely, described as hyperactive, and my growing serenity was something that just seemed to happen without me even noticing. Looking back, I can see what a perfect match Richard and I were, and how much his own calming and yet surprisingly forceful energy could not help but affect mine. It was the love between us that was forever sensitive to each other's needs; our only wish being to make each other happy. I didn't know I had ever been truly unhappy and yet the union I shared with him had made me question the qualities of happiness. Maybe we sometimes use the word inappropriately? Maybe, *happiness* has a different meaning for each of us? It would be a long way into self-enquiry before understanding that happiness is our natural state of being – that only our mind can choose to experience, or reject. No body and no thing can make us happy or unhappy.

When we eventually arrived back in England, it was the end of January and very cold. We hadn't anticipated the effect this might have on our four month old baby who had experienced little other than the warm sun in her short life so far. Katy temporarily stopped breathing, her little lungs responding to the shock of the freezing air that she inhaled as we walked from the warm airport out into the cold night. Our happy, contented baby promptly registered her disdain of the way she was being treated, by chastising her shocked parents with a somewhat noisy protest!

How lovely it was to be home again, much as we missed our

friends. My family and friends in England hadn't even met Katy yet and we couldn't wait to introduce her to everyone. Everything seemed unreal and it took me a while to take the reality of what had been happening in the last months on board. Perhaps I had subconsciously tried to pretend the worst parts were just a dream. I had come home, but my dad was not there; in the two years we had been in Kuwait I had lost no less than three members of my family, the other two being aunts who had both played significant roles in my life. But it was the death of my father that would hit me (if not immediately) and later, I would realize that I hadn't even had the opportunity to grieve for him. Somehow it was always unfinished business that I would attend to when the time was right, but I postponed it for a long time. It was just too painful to address and whilst I didn't know it at the time, there would be more pressing issues than indulging in my own grief. The passing of my father, the questions I can never ask him now, let alone hear the answers, and my awareness of his inability to even mention death, has made me appreciate how inadequately my culture addresses an inevitable process in our lives – by virtually denying its certainty. We cannot experience life to our full potential until we begin to accept that our death is as much a part of life and as significant as our physical birth. Our disinclination to acknowledge death as a new beginning or another dimension of life, rather than the end and final part of our mere physical existence, makes our lives meaningless and without purpose. Not only do we greet our own advancing years with sadness and fear, but tend to dismiss the elders as a problem rather than an asset in our society. The much-revered elders of other cultures, however, are frequently from families within countries already truly burdened by economic deprivation. How uncomfortable does that make us feel? We need to start discussing and addressing preparation for death as much as we talk endlessly about our life issues and plans. The opportunity to experience life in a physical body is all in the preparation of our greatest celebration of all – when we step out of our body and return *home* once more, a much richer soul. Let us anticipate our own parting with joy and wonderment and let us also celebrate the physical life of our loved ones, as they merely step into a new dimension. We constantly teach our children the values and rewards of hard work and diligence, enforcing the belief that life is all about getting a good job, earning a good salary and bettering ourselves against others. We tell our children nothing about the real purpose of life and the real values of fully experiencing themselves in life; of understanding fearlessly what they really came to achieve; of knowing that *achievement* is measured by one's best effort, not a piece of gold in the hand. We tell our children nothing about true goals in life because *we* so often, fail to grasp that truth ourselves.

Coming home to the UK was almost as much a culture shock as first arriving in the Middle East. Just the understanding that we no longer had to stockpile certain foods any more took some adjustment. Even today, I find it difficult not to take advantage of a substantial store of my favourite foods, almost as if they will disappear off the shelves for good. Rediscovering the prices of household items in England compared with the very expensive prices in Kuwait was yet another revelation that became quite a costly one. When shopping for furniture and such like, we were so elated to be able to find what we wanted that we seemed quite unperturbed by the inflated British prices. It was, for instance, sometime before we realized that the thousand pounds we paid for a new bed was quite excessive and, frankly, not good value for money either! In Kuwait we would probably have paid three times that amount for the same thing, but it was a while before we stopped using that ludicrous comparison as a measure of a bargain or not.

As I sit and write sharing an overview of my life, I am somewhat interested in the choice of my own recollections and, indeed, the emotions that are still evoked from these memories. It often seems that the more unpleasant experiences in my life, although not losing their significance in my memory, frequently tend to become less painful with the passage of time. Positive, happy experiences on the other hand seem to be recalled retaining the full impact of their occurrence and can always be relied upon to uplift and generate further joy. Many endure the most horrendous experiences in life and their memories rarely lose their sting, yet, despite the pain and suffering at the time, many have gone on to lead fulfilled and joyous lives, often using their past as a stepping stone to a new beginning.

Unfortunately we don't usually have any warning of the rough parts of life, and even when we do, there is often a tendency to take it for what it is rather than seek to discover what it may be teaching us. I think I was in that category; never really wanting to believe that my body was working anything less than perfectly and equally as disbelieving of the effects of the stress I was subjecting it to.

The word *stress* is one that most of us now believe to be a necessary evil in our lives, even though the adverse effects on our bodies are scientifically proven. It seems that we are more prepared to deal with the after-effects of the stress than eliminate its cause, perhaps reflecting our inability to identify its cause in the first place. I frequently have people coming for healing saying that they need help because they are stressed – as if it is some sort of disease that can be treated medically, or otherwise.

Many of us are unaware of the effects of stress on our bodies and even if we are, we probably believe there is little we can do about it. Those of us with stressful lifestyles and jobs wrongly believe that our only option to avoid its uncomfortable effects is to change the course of our career. Clearly, this is not a solution and many of us who find a highly demanding job stressful are equally likely to find one that is less demanding still as stressful. Stress *is* under our control, but at the end of the day we may decide to just walk away, saying enough is enough. Before taking such drastic action, however, we should first examine the nature of its cause and, even more significantly, our own reaction to it. Stress is a word without meaning for some of us, supporting my belief that it is merely a word that describes the negative reaction that some of us have to certain situations. If we place tension on a piece of elastic for a long duration, the elastic will lose its elasticity and thus its function. Primarily resisting the constant pulling at either end, it finally submits to the stress imposed on it. Alas, the piece of elastic has no choice; it is stressed beyond its purpose or capability.

Few of us want to acknowledge that our disabled bodies may be the result of the long-term (or even short-term) stress we have imposed on it, much rather knowing that a virus or some other recognizable and treatable medical condition is responsible for our discomfort. Frequently, of course, a diagnosed disease may be blamed for our symptoms, but the root cause of our suscepti-bility to it in the first place is often left unattended. We may be treated with drugs or even surgery, which hopefully assists in our recovery, but unless we are also able to diagnose and attend to the real cause, nature will undoubtedly catch up with us once more. Anyone who has done any interior decorating will know that just plastering over the cracks is a soul-destroying job and unless they are channelled out to the root and filled in accord-ingly, the defects will reappear within a very short time. It is part of a nurse's training to know that it is vital for a deep wound such as an abscess to be encouraged to heal from the base. When healing is allowed to rapidly take place on the surface, the under-lying crater, silently and unsuspectingly, festers – before erupting yet again. The former procedure may take considerably longer than the latter, but it's the only way to ensure complete healing.

Chapter Nine

Quietly observing and recalling, in retrospect, my body had been protesting for quite a while, but its gentler warnings had fallen upon deaf ears. When we don't want to hear something, the easiest way out for us is to pretend it wasn't said in the first place. Before we are finally forced to accept the message, we become so used to hearing it repeated so many times that we push the boundaries even more, believing we can risk just one more warning before taking action. It's rather like the child who almost taunts his elders with his repeated defiance of their instruction, until they finally snap and serve the punishment. Unfortunately, I didn't know, any more than the child, just when the final warning had been given, before it was too late. I would like to say that I didn't have any idea of the consequences, but that would be slightly untrue; it was always going to be tomorrow when I would slow down and re-evaluate the way I was treating my body. So – I wasn't drinking or on drugs, I was just so addicted to adrenalin that I couldn't (or *thought* I couldn't) do without it. Drug addicts need money to support their addiction, but all I needed was the stress that created it and, like any addict, the best time to decide to kick the habit is when you've just had your *fix* and are on a *high*. Like any other stimulant that we may use, knowingly or not, it has a very limited value and is only effective short term. On the contrary, apart from losing its positive potential through overuse, its constant high levels in our body results in irreversible damage and just the opposite effect to that which we'd desired.

How dramatic this all sounds. It was unfortunately, and I came close to testing my belief of a life hereafter because of it. It's rare for the medical profession to link an identified and treatable disease with the stress that caused it, let alone identify the real nature of stress. My comments here are not of criticism but observations – observations that remind me, who really is responsible for our own well-being. Interestingly, it's also easy to attribute a patient's symptoms to something like stress, having failed to establish an organic disease. Unfortunately, although most doctors suffer it – that's not usually the word used to account for a patient's physical malfunction because it can rarely be scientifically validated. More readily, medication is prescribed to 'raise the mood', in the belief that the cause of the symptoms is due to a depressed mind rather than an ill functioning body due to something we cannot understand.

Our expectation of the medical profession has always surpassed what is reasonable or fair, and has allowed us to delegate our own responsibilities. Why should a doctor be expected to diagnose beyond his or her own domain? It is only in recent years that the Western world has turned to what is frequently regarded as alternative or complementary therapies to make us feel better. There is of course quite a difference between *alternative*, which is literally – 'another way' and *complementary*, which suggests 'supporting' or, in addition to. Why do we so wrongly believe that a doctor must have all the answers for us and why – do we then put all our faith in another therapy, when he fails to meet our expectations?

I know that traditional medicine can be a lifesaver and I for one owe my life to its expertise. We only have to observe parts of the world that don't enjoy the health care that we do in the West to appreciate how fortunate we are. However, there are areas in the world which have not only taught us the essence and application of what we call alternative therapies, but are themselves dependent on these ancient traditions. It is interesting that these cultures don't just offer herbal elixirs to be ingested or applied. Their innate understanding of the causes of all ill health is reflected in their holistic healing of the mind, body and spirit; as indeed was practised by the first great physician of true medicine, Hippocrates himself.

Our loss of faith in traditional medicine has led us to seek out many alternative routes which have now become a lucrative industry. Before blindly cutting ourselves off from one in favour of another, perhaps we should enquire of ourselves what we really are seeking; lest we become dissatisfied once more. Do we really have to make a choice? Until the unlikely event of doctors and scientists linking our energetic and physical well-being, they will continue to fail to provide us with holistic healing, but we should also remind ourselves who it was who designated that role to them. Healing is not something that just happens, regardless of the 'physician' we seek to help us – the journey is ours and our responsibility alone.

Many people ask me why, gifted as a healer, I have suffered so much with my own health issues. I often feel the enquiry being made is a kind of judgment and have to admit that, I have no idea. As my own quest progresses, I find as many questions that are answered, there are still more keeping their silence. The question that people put to me is not of course one of judgment but a compassionate enquiry, whilst at the same time seeking answers for their own deeper questions. To understand the answers completely we need to accept that life is a spiritual journey and to comprehend its role in the *true* nature of healing. But for that we must first unveil the causes of much of our human suffering – and this is where my journey begins. We are ready to suggest that a rare miracle has occurred when someone survives something that, interestingly, has also been attributed to *God's* will. If our cancer or heart attack was *God's* will – why did *God* decide to perform a miracle to save us? Calling something a *miracle* automatically acknowledges its rarity – doesn't it? But are miracles really as rare as we think and if not – what is the meaning of the word? The more attentive I've become over the years to my spiritual quest, the more certain I've become that there is only one miracle – the *miracle of life* itself. When we see ourselves and every other living organism as an integral part of life, we may also understand that there are no miracles – just life. What more could we want? How could we ever believe that anything could surpass such perfection? Have we forgotten the miracle of the very body we inhabit, built from millions of individual cells functioning faultlessly within its own singular unit, and yet so magnificently designed to combine forces to form the essential matrix of our physical existence? Each minute cell, maintaining its own equilibrium whilst joining other cells, to create the most beautiful orchestra of functional organ systems, directed – by an imperceptible intelligence, in order to maintain the perfect balance and harmony of the human organism. Is that not the *true* miracle – *the miracle that – Is* – as we witness our own *Being*?

I make no apology for repetition in my writing. I have already said that it has been through repetition that my most valuable lessons have been delivered and the greatest rocks upturned to reveal the wisdom beneath them. We may think we are making progress, believing we have answers to the deeper meaning of life, but before being allowed to become too comfortable, we are thrown off balance again by yet a stronger wave. As we attempt to restore our shaky equilibrium, even greater challenges are presented to us and even bigger questions posed, until we finally ask the most crucial one of all – 'just *who* – is the questioner here?'

Chapter Ten

The first year back in the UK wasn't too bad since our young baby was more than accommodating when I needed rest. I don't know how he managed it but night feeds and diaper changing seemed to become second nature to Richard, and despite having to fly off to some far off land in the less respectable hours of night, he would always make sure he carried out his duties before leaving! Many a time I had heard a cooing babe, engrossed in conversation with her daddy. Never was there a murmur of discontent or resentment from him; on the contrary, his role as second time father was one he revelled in and his undivided love for me, too, totally accepted the way things were. He became my strength and I became his, and that bond would get stronger and stronger, until it was inseparable.

Shortly before Katy's second birthday, at a time that I was beginning to anticipate the future with optimism, I needed further surgery. Unsettling thoughts went through my mind as I was faced with the cruel reality of what was happening. Each evening Richard would put our two year old in her child seat at the rear of the car and head up the M40 for thirty miles – just to visit Mummy for an hour or so. I was feeling like a part-time mother and, at most, a part-time wife. I began to wonder if Katy would end up suffering from maternal deprivation. However absurd I now understand these thoughts were, they were very real at the time, as I am reminded of their stronghold. When I left hospital I felt I was witnessing someone else's life, not my own. I reflected on all the people I had nursed during my career in similar circumstances and, although I was never insensitive, I wanted to find them again and tell them that now I *really* understand how they had perhaps felt.

The next two years (the preschool years) were so delightful, watching with amazement as any other parent, the development of our child. Much of the time seemed to be spent going backwards and forwards for hospital appointments, as the doctors tried to establish whatever was happening to my body at that time. Many were the days on this long and painful journey when I just wanted to stop and enjoy what I had. And I did have a lot to be grateful for. I was gifted with not only a beautiful child but was surrounded by the love and support of a devoted husband, not to mention family and friends; a gift that so many envy.

We always seem to want more, never seemingly satisfied or accepting of what we have, and I was no exception as I yearned to be a real mum – one who could run and chase and lift and swim. How cruel it seemed at the time when I realized that Richard was such a better playmate than me, and yet, young Katy still knew where to come when her ears were throbbing or her throat was sore. She knew we were still a team and I was very much part of it, with a very important role. It was almost as if she was programmed just to know.

As the months progressed, Katy didn't need to draw on any hidden source of understanding about every one's role in the household; it was all too clear, but apparently fun too. During the frequent episodes when I was unable to stay erect any longer, a little girl – always ready to execute a routine she had rehearsed many times with her father – caringly ushered me to the settee. Shoes off, blanket, a cushion for my head and, as soon as I was feeling stronger, out went the orders to Daddy to put the kettle on. Richard worked tirelessly to maintain optimism and fun – a precious legacy passed on to our daughter.

Chapter Eleven

It's strange when you look back on a certain period of your life. What seemed intolerable at the time tends to fade into just a recollection, and yet that realization alone has helped me immeasurably. Time and time again I have been thrown into the abyss, knowing that finally I would reach the bottom where there would be no further to fall. Such a journey is not of course peculiar to me and many will visit the depths, but it's the darkness that pervades which prevents us from noticing others on the same journey. Ultimately, knowing that there is no further to fall becomes a great opportunity of growth and understanding because there are only two options for us to choose from. We can stay in the darkness at the bottom of the chasm or search for the light and head on upwards towards it as it guides us. The climb is always difficult but the light gets stronger with our ascent, until we can finally see where we are heading.

I didn't reach the bottom too many times but sometimes it was just too difficult to save myself. I can remember feeling as though I were clinging to the tufts of grass on a cliff edge, knowing how very easy it would be just to let go and let myself effortlessly fall. Whilst I never contemplated ending my own life, I feel so compassionate towards others and their ultimate submission to their own intolerable suffering. I feel blessed that life hasn't challenged me enough to consider its only alternative as the way to free myself from pain, but many are not so fortunate and, in their dark, lonely hours of despair, decide that dying is a preferable choice to living. None of us can know how high up the mountain we can climb – until we reach that point on our ascent.

I always believed that if I had a clear understanding of what was happening to my body everything would somehow be alright, more tolerable. What a strange thought. Having had major gastric surgery and all the subsequent problems that it created – I was now able to account for my years of previous pain and symptoms, but it now seemed that I was looking for other answers and was either trusting enough or naïve to expect any quick responses.

Katy was approaching her fourth birthday and by now my ability to function on an acceptable level was greatly unpredictable. Frequently we all sat in the car ready to drive off somewhere, before all plans had to be rapidly changed. Every grain of energy suddenly and without warning left my muscles, making it impossible for me to sit, let alone stand on two feet.

It's surprising what you get used to and call *normal*. It's as though you keep changing gear and as long as you change down in time, the engine doesn't groan too much. I don't know why, but the worst times for me were always the various investigations followed by the anticipation of the results. Although some were pretty uncomfortable I mainly accepted them as part of the course, for which I might have anticipated a positive outcome. It was the long periods of hospitalization that I came to dread because these stays resulted, yet again, in false hope and seemingly pointless separation from the family. These were the times when my frustration led to an inner anger and deep resentment. I felt as though I could hold myself together no longer as I inwardly screamed for help. But as has always been my journey, help would be given in whatever way was needed to somehow guide or support me to the next stage. I always found that after the initial shock or disappointment, after which I would fall helplessly through the darkness of the abyss once more, there was always a chink of light showing me which way to go. It was rather like the eyes' adjustment to a dark room or place. It seemed pitch black at first, until my eyes became accustomed to the reality of my surroundings – removing all fear of the scary shadows. How many times do we find ourselves in this place? How often do we react to the first impact of information that hits our brain? But the damage is done, even though we have discovered our fear to be unfounded and the figure hiding behind the door – a figment of our imagination. It is only when we learn to experience the present moment as it arrives, rather than allowing our minds to fill in the gaps and jump to the next scenario, that we become in tune with life. There *is* nothing other than the present moment; a moment that we are alive or the moment in which we may leave our physical existence, but in truth, the only part of our living – of any value – of any importance. So we shouldn't throw it away and regret missing out on its beauty.

'It's a miracle!' Well we all thought so but it had taken Richard a good week to believe it. After three days of hydrocortisone, I was nearly a new woman. I could feel it in my body like a little infectious light that energized every part of it. I was beginning to feel as I hadn't felt for the past five or more years, but Richard's first reaction alarmed me greatly. I was shocked and upset when at first he failed to share my optimism and my joy. I began to wonder if he felt my new found energy would somehow threaten our relationship. His behaviour was so unlike him. I questioned my own reactions because I had always been fiercely independent and knew that I grieved its absence more than anything over the past few years. As I anticipated my new life, I was at the same time sensitive to Richard's needs too. He had always been so perceptive of mine; always acknowledging my strengths as a person, mother, and wife, whilst regarding my growing physical weakness as – "*noise on the system*," as he so succinctly put it. As much as I wanted to say – 'But it's not you it's happening to', I never did. I never did because I knew that my suffering was his suffering too and that his approach to life was as strengthening to me as mine apparently was to him.

Maybe those few uncomfortable days, when I was almost questioning the physical changes I was feeling in my body before Richard would acknowledge it, was yet another lesson for me. However, I didn't have too long to wait to understand his delayed reactions and concurrently experience his sheer explosion of joy – as he became the first to tell everyone! We had just taken a wonderful walk by the river and I had returned, still with energy to spare. As if to check the truth of this miracle I went straight to the kitchen to make us a cup of tea. I came back, bypassing the settee, but setting up the ironing board. Richard was missing. He could contain his joy no longer and had begun to work his way through a list of phone calls, starting with my mother. It became very evident that he just hadn't allowed himself to believe what was happening, for all our sakes, but could he really think it was a figment of imagination any more? If it was a placebo effect, as I suspect he first wondered, I would have been delighted. I had been given a new beginning and that's all I could ever ask for.

Chapter Twelve

Katy's fourth birthday was really a time for celebration for more reasons than one. Richard was made an offer he couldn't refuse and had decided to take early retirement to help me and enjoy Katy's last year, before starting school. Just then we didn't know quite how precious that time together would be, but thankfully we enjoyed it to the full. As previously promised, I *allowed* Richard to have a cat now that he was available to rescue all the mice and birds that it would no doubt offer us. I sadly, whilst loving all animals, had a fear of cats that I'd never come to terms with, but my introduction to Ming and Fred was going to cure me of that, forever! These two beautiful Burmese siblings understood my every need and I have never looked back – as the RSPCA will verify! All perfectly planned to coincide with each other came another addition to the family when our beloved Border collie joined us. After dedicated training, Meg truly did become our best friend – guarding and protecting all whom she believed to be in her pack.

What a wonderful four years. I still needed to pace myself once I understood I wasn't going to be able to live on the constant *high* before my cortisone levels stabilized, but that didn't matter; we were finally enjoying so many things that I previously hadn't been able to do. One Sunday, we had gone to have lunch with some friends, taking a stroll in the nearby wildlife park in the afternoon. The entrance to the park was gained through a sort of garden centre, but it wasn't the plants that attracted my interest. Over one hour later, never having stepped foot in the park, Richard and I had parted with over a thousand pounds, having bought a trailer tent. The strange thing is that I had never even heard of such things before, but it was a visit that none of us ever regretted. We were now free agents to just pack up and go, whenever we pleased. The novice campers were about to embark on a wonderful new experience and subscribe a few laughs for observers on the way!

We went just about everywhere in that tent. After a few mishaps (which included Richard releasing our mobile water carrier into someone's barbeque at the bottom of the hill), we quickly became professional campers and soon preferred sleeping under the stars to the comfort of our home. Another tent was almost permanently erected in our garden during the summer months. Living outside, away from the television and ringing telephone, is wonderful enough, but something much deeper and long lasting is experienced. I always felt as though I was, not just in harmony with the stars and the night sky, but part of it, *essential* to it. Even now, when I take a night stroll outside to let the dog out, I look up at the stars and the moon and feel as though they are speaking to me. As I close my door and go back to bed, I remember where I really want to be, where I feel most at peace and at *one* with myself and the universe around me. I look back on these memories with fond recollection, but in truth, there are no words to express the emotions that touch the heart of one's soul. As I ponder on the words I write, I am at peace with an inner wisdom. My emotions have no influence on my soul but are the energetic expression of the beautiful harmony and *oneness* that my soul has revealed to me. Although I didn't know it at the time, these very, very, precious years – would be short lived. Thank goodness we crammed so much into them.

Katy had her own new adventures when she started at the local primary school. I remained well enough to join her on occasions both as a helping mother and, later, as an employed assistant for children with special needs for a few hours a week. I find young children so rewarding to work with, regardless of their history. All have exactly the same basic needs but some just shout louder than others to have them met, often resulting in their needs being sadly misinterpreted. It's amazing how children respond to being treated and respected as an equal human being, even at that young age. Unfortunately, this seems to be something that adults frequently pay lip service to but fail to practise. Right from the start, so many of us misguidedly believe that discipline is just about control, rather than nurture. Any animal feeling it is being controlled will try to break loose somehow or other. It may be possible to teach a dog to 'walk to heel' but if he learns through love and kindness, the lesson is one of team-ship and respect; if he learns by fear, the lesson is one of fear and resentment. Either way, your dog will have learnt obedience, but according to your needs – to have control, rather than your dog – *being in control*. A dog that learns through love and kindness is learning like Pavlov's dog – he knows what is expected of him to receive that response. When we learn through love and kindness, we respond quickly to our lessons, but more importantly, we become loving, kind adults, because we know no other way to be.

When we examine the fundamental differences in dog training, it may give us food for thought, but don't most of us assume a *right* to control others? No? Don't we want others to conform to our way of living – thinking – behaving? More often than not, we don't have the ability to actually control others in the way we may a dog, but we do have a pretty good try. I'm not suggesting that we all condone clearly unacceptable behaviour but we need to question not only what it is that is unacceptable, but why it is. Maybe we would be surprised or even shocked to discover how often our judgment, or even hatred, has its causal roots in our own need to control and change things to our own liking. Parents very often don't question the demands they put on their children, past an excuse that – 'That's how we were brought up'. Search inside your own mind now and see – how much of your own living pattern is based on unquestioned beliefs and conditioning?

We don't have to be a grade 'A' scholar to perceive the effects of unchallenged beliefs on global harmony. How often do we recognize the grossly inaccurate representation of people of another culture, country, religion or political party, largely based on the need of a few to have control – *to have and abuse power*? We must be ready to examine the origins of our frequently unfounded beliefs. Even if at first we find difficulty in changing the habits of a lifetime, let us at least start to respect the beliefs of others, because the gift of acceptance of one another unveils the ultimate truth – we seek in ourselves.

Many people who knew Richard and me frequently commented, with a hint of envy perhaps, on our unique or special relationship. I don't know if our relationship was any more unique than any relationship, but it was certainly very precious to both of us and therefore special. If you are unfamiliar with something, I suppose there's a danger of believing it is unique because it seems different, but I sometimes found these comments disturbing. When we see something that perhaps we would like ourselves, there is always a tendency to assume it came readymade – especially when it is a relationship, but also regarding others' achievements. What we often don't know is that however perfect something seems, it usually has to be earned and worked at to keep it that way. Nothing is ever static in life and that includes all relationships we have during our living experience. A relationship can only move two ways – up or down, but it can never stay unchanged; it must either grow or it must slowly begin to die – the latter occurring frequently when one or both partners fails to feed the fire and keep it alive. It's difficult for one partner to do this on his or her own, regardless of their dedication, but the whole essence of any relationship should be the balance of giving and taking between the two within it. We are all unique and how better could this be demonstrated than in our very own DNA? In our understanding of our individuality we must also accept that we cannot predict or judge another's thoughts or actions in accordance with our own. Although we may seem the same on the surface, just like the DNA – there are many hidden variables. Our expectancy of another's behaviour leads to judgment, which is directly akin to our need, yet again, to control another human being.

All relationships in life, however we perceive them, give us the gift of another opportunity to grow. Even animals provide a chance for us to discover a part of ourselves that we were not previously in touch with. I have met so many people who have been quite indifferent to animals until they finally submitted to the pleas of their children and discovered the magic of owning one. My own deep respect for all animals has grown from childhood when, at the time, I valued the bond with my dog more than my human family. At least we seemed to understand each other. Not allowing children interaction with animals is denying them a privileged opportunity that in turn will benefit the world. I have worked with children so damaged by their previous experiences in life and yet who have related remarkably to animals. Animals respond so rewardingly to love which in turn, teaches a child respect for nature, even when human relationships and ties break down. Animals don't judge us; they just accept us as we are – connected by the common essence of *who* we are.

Chapter Thirteen

Having retired for three years, Richard was made another offer he couldn't refuse. The company was expanding into the Far East and he was asked to oversee its launching. Actually, we were all very excited about his new post because he'd already decided to take us with him on one of his visits. I have always wanted to visit the countries he was involved with: Japan, India, China, Singapore and Hong Kong, but the pictures he had already come back with and the stories he related just whetted our appetite and anticipation even more.

"OK, darling – I'll have the kettle on."

Although he was very fond of a somewhat stronger drink, my husband was always ready for a cup of tea. When Katy was at school, we seemed to drink gallons of it before realizing that it was lunchtime and we still hadn't stopped talking! But today was different. He had called me from the office to say that he was on his way home and would pick up his flight tickets on the way. The following day he was due to fly out to Singapore for a meeting. Everything was ready and we would have a quiet meal together that evening, before he went. That was the plan anyway.

I heard the car coming up the drive sooner than I'd anticipated and Katy had run down the stairs in excitement, but that soon changed. As I saw the outline of Richard's figure behind the glass kitchen door, all I felt was alarm bells ringing. This man who had been laughing and joking with me just an hour before was standing at the door, shaking, sweating, and with a distinct blue tinge to his pale shocked complexion. I was very alarmed and hastened to usher him in – convinced that he was having a heart attack. There were times when I found my husband exceedingly difficult, as I did then, when I reached for the phone to ring the ambulance. Other than to say that I was frightened of making him worse by arguing, I have no idea to this day why I didn't just go ahead with what clearly was the sensible thing to do. Maybe it was something to do with the simultaneous phone call that came just as I was about to take control. It was my mother's doctor on the line telling me that she had just been taken into hospital again and that, this time – he felt her battle was waning.

My dearest wish was to be with my mother when she eventually passed on. I had actually promised her in all good faith that she wouldn't die alone. Mother, a smoker for as many years as I can remember, had paid the price; suffering with emphysema for almost as many. We'd had so many false alarms over the years when she had panicked or had an exacerbation that we felt entitled to believe she would live to celebrate her oncoming seventieth birthday. The memories of those hours are still almost too painful to revisit. Richard was insisting that I go to my mother (two hours away) because he knew I would otherwise regret it. Did this man not understand how ill he was or, indeed, what his appearance was like?

I didn't go to my mother and she died, twenty-four hours later. I still hope she understood why, but it seems so unfair that I was denied the opportunity to be with her and to have broken my promise. Was I denied it? This is a question I have asked so many times, but in the end, it is only I who has the answer. I had a choice but I will never know if I made the best one, considering the limited information at the time.

Richard didn't have a heart attack. How relieved we all were. The doctor said he had a renal infection and was in need of a prostatectomy. After some antibiotics, he was anxious to see a surgeon and get it over and done with to enable him to get back to work and his meetings in the Far East. I had unfortunately remembered nursing patients after this surgery during my training and was not at all happy to hear the plan. After seeing the surgeon, arrangements were made for Richard's operation the following week, after which, I learnt to my horror, he would spend three nights in hospital and then go back to work after a week's rest at home! This was just all too much for me to digest.

Chapter Fourteen

Well, clearly, I was not up to date with the latest treatment, which was hardly surprising since my own speciality was paediatrics. With no side effects at all and within ten days of surgery we were at Heathrow saying goodbye, yet again. This time, his destination was India and he anticipated being there for at least two weeks. It was quite an adventure really because we had made many Indian friends whilst in the Middle East and it would be nice for Richard to be able to relate to the many stories they told us about their lives in India. These people not only have a very kind disposition but also a great sense of humour, which certainly matched Richard's. There were times when I have seen their previously puzzled faces burst into laughter as they realized he was yet again – 'pulling their leg'. Humour and laughter is so important in life and yet I still don't know if it is something we learn or just part of our genes. He seemed capable of turning anything into a joke and to see the funny side to any situation, which I found frustrating on occasions, repeatedly begging him to be serious, for just a moment. I have always loved to laugh although I'm not quick-witted; unlike my daughter who seems to have inherited the gift from both her father and maternal grandfather.

Well, never was humour needed more than it was then. I had received the usual phone call from Richard – just to check-in with us and speak to Katy, who was now keenly plotting his journey on a map as he travelled. She was now nearly eight and India was a place that we would all visit when this particular assignment had been completed, so there was a lot of excitement and anticipation. Richard told me he may not be able to ring for two or three days which was quite understandable and yet, for some reason – I didn't feel easy. Two days later I got another call, but this time to say that his schedule had changed and he would be coming home early. I should have been as excited as Katy, but mine was cloaked in what seemed a completely unfounded anxiety. Unfortunately, I had long known that such feelings would not be unfounded – I had experienced too many of them.

And this was no exception. How long can you entertain a sleepy-eyed youngster in an airport at five, six, and seven in the morning? Without warning, the flight was nearly three hours late and I began to worry about the nature of my anxiety. Finally, waiting expectantly the first passengers came up through the barriers, but there was no sign of my husband. I thought my racing heart would explode – until at last, I recognized his suitcase, but before I could react, Katy could contain herself no more. Unaware that she had entered the security zone, I saw her speeding excitedly into her father's arms, or at least... that's what she expected to happen, but this time was different. I still have a lump in my throat as I try to find the words to describe this scenario. Richard was grey, and I don't mean his hair. He was very tired and was obviously sick, but I didn't know in what way. As Katy approached him in her normal exuberant manner, he put his hands up to stop her coming any closer. I pray that one day that scene will be softened... if not erased from my memory altogether.

It wasn't long before we were speeding down the motorway to home. Richard was trying desperately to maintain humour and normality for Katy's sake, but she knew that all was not well. We knew that there would be no bottle of wine to crack open in celebration of his homecoming that evening. The journey back to Marlow was time enough for me to understand that the surgery had not been radical enough, resulting in the agonizing pain he endured. Suddenly, unable to empty his bladder and somehow believing that it was due to dehydration, Richard had taken things into his own hands by encouraging the natural process with a few cans of beer! The contrast of emotions I feel between the last scenario and this one is indeed a contrast. Although I felt desperately sorry for his situation, I can never believe that an intelligent, informed man could draw such a conclusion about his own anatomy. I didn't let him live it down for a long time. The poor chap, however, with a near exploding bladder writhed in a hotel room in the middle of Bombay. When he eventually got help for himself, he was told that the specialist was not currently in the local hospital so he would be taken across town to another hospital. Anyone familiar with the nature of Indian taxis and the roads they drive on – may sympathetically cringe. No wonder he didn't think he was going to survive the journey. Richard met with nothing but kindness in India and despite the meagre hospital facilities he couldn't fault the expert care he received and consideration shown to him. The only way to bypass the offending obstruction was by putting a catheter directly into his bladder wall; an alarming procedure for him I imagine, but also one of instant relief. No wonder he was so reticent to respond to Katy's enthusiastic welcome.

At least I now understood my intuitive anxiety which had, thankfully, since gone away – for a while anyway. It's strange how much can happen in a short time, but even stranger how the mind struggles to make it somewhat less painful afterwards. I know that we had all attended my mother's funeral shortly around Richard's first surgery, but how he managed to fit it in, I still can't recall. I have a perfect recollection of the days following his second operation though.

I rang the surgeon as soon as we got back from the airport, only to find that he was in the process of loading his car in preparation for a family skiing trip. I went to his house to collect a letter of referral to another surgeon in Oxford. When I arrived, he was just strapping the skis to the roof rack and I couldn't help thinking how much nicer it would be for Richard to be taking to the mountains, rather than into an operating theatre. 'What bad timing' – I thought. It seemed such bad luck that the two events were happening at exactly the same time, and yet, in some weird way, it was probably the most fortuitous thing that could have happened, as I say – in some weird way.

It was a strange feeling returning to Oxford where I had lived, worked, and spent many anxious times in the outpatient clinics myself. Much to my relief, I knew the surgeon now in charge of Richard's second operation, which was certainly comforting. I was also comforted by his instructions to Richard regarding his next trip to the Far East, but although agreeing not to step foot out of the country in less than two weeks after surgery, I knew he had other thoughts in mind.

Within the next twenty-four hours Richard was recovering from his surgery, but this time it was unexpectedly slow. I knew there was something wrong but the doctors tried to convince me that everything was quite in order – "Two doses of anaesthesia within such a short time is bound to slow things down a bit," they said. But I wasn't convinced that the grumbling discomfort he had in his abdomen could be explained away so simply as – 'Accumulating gas, after the anaesthesia'. He was discharged home three days after the surgery. What do you do with *feelings* that will not go away but can neither be rationalized?

Eventually, you will be forced to act on them. Within the next twenty-four hours I was calling the doctor out to see my husband, in a lot of pain. I had no doubt what the problem was and suddenly understood the cause of the sporadic bouts of what he had always considered 'dietary indiscretions'. So here was a chap who had made no visits to his doctor other than an insurance check-up now facing his third operation within less than eight weeks. Perhaps he was making up for all the attention I owed him, we used to banter. Richard was quick to get back on his feet after the antibiotics dealt with the infection, but it would be necessary to have the stone-impacted gallbladder removed. He was in his usual hurry to get things moving and had a deadline for an important meeting he was chairing, this time in Beijing. He had done his research and knew that with keyhole surgery (which was still quite a new procedure at the time) he could be in and out virtually overnight. Can you imagine how perfectly jinxed he felt when he learnt that the specialist in this particular procedure had just gone on leave and wouldn't be back for three weeks, by which time his own conference would have been and gone. Actually, without him – there would be no conference. I can't remember how long Richard hung on to the belief that he would still be able to make it to China, but then... it doesn't really matter now.

Chapter Fifteen

The surgery was booked and a friend took Katy to school whilst I drove Richard to the hospital. He'd been instructed to fast for the previous twelve hours so he could have his surgery that day. But something was wrong – different. We were both uncharacteristically edgy with each other, which I remember feeling quite hurt about. That was perhaps nothing compared to the hurt I would feel when he told me not to hang around waiting with him, because that again was such an unusual request. A lump in my throat, I respected his wishes, drove home and sat down to a cup of coffee – but not before responding to a feeling that urged me to ring his room. Neither of us had been able to account for the way we were feeling, even more so our reactions to them, but we'd had the opportunity to talk and leave each other in a much lighter and positive mood.

I was so pleased that I had phoned but the feelings didn't go away, and I didn't know why. The surgery should be relatively straightforward so maybe I just wasn't used to seeing my best friend and partner poorly. Anyway, I would soon ring the ward when he was back from theatre and hopefully go to see him that night. I collected Katy from school then gave the ward a ring, but there was no news as yet because the operating list had apparently been delayed. Poor darling – he wasn't the most patient person at the best of times. In the meantime, I gave Katy her dinner and got her ready for bed before ringing again, but this time I was told that Richard's operation had been so delayed that he hadn't returned from the recovery ward yet. All this made perfect sense to me because, as a nurse, I knew that theatre lists rarely go to plan. All you need is one emergency to put it back for hours, but something was very uncomfortable inside me. I had felt it for a few days but it was now reaching a crescendo.

Having seen Katy to bed, I enquired again about Richard, but I knew now that I was being fobbed off when I was told that the surgeon would ring after his list had finished. By this time it was gone eight at night and I lost my cool, insisting that I be told the truth. I didn't have to wait much longer before the surgeon was explaining that apart from removing the gallbladder, he had also taken a malignant tumour from Richard's colon. The surgeon was quick to point out how fortuitous it was that he had not had keyhole surgery since the cancer certainly wouldn't have been discovered. Having expressed my gratitude and put the phone down, I saw a dark black curtain descending – as though the show was over and the theatre closed. I will never forget that moment. It seemed that all our plans and aspirations had been devoured by this horrible dark place that I couldn't get out of. I knew now that Richard wasn't waiting for another patient to come out of surgery; it was he who was holding them all up.

But I had to get out of that place, and as I sat on the floor numbed to my core I saw the same black curtain lifting again. I had to be strong now – stronger than I'd ever needed to be before and as I sent out my prayers for 'reinforcements', so was I magically energized. To this day, I could never describe either my feelings at the time or the miracle that seemed to have taken place. I was still struggling with my own health issues but we had a young child who needed us both. I now had to find the strength and energy to fill in all the gaps.

Nothing could have prepared me for Richard's appearance the following day, even though I had nursed many sick people like him. Even worse was the attitude of the nurses who, although very kind, seemed to think my husband was their property. I have never asked a close relative to go out of the room whilst an intravenous infusion was being changed or a face being sponged. I was shocked, angry, and very hurt but didn't know how to express any of it. Richard was grey and in a semi-coma – probably not even knowing I was there. As I sat holding his hand and watching him, I was suddenly aware that his breathing was irregular and periodically stopped completely. I was alerted to the morphine pump he had running into a vein and, recognizing the side effects, knew he was having too much, but the difficulties in getting the nurses to agree was harrowing. It wasn't until I rang later that day that I was told that – my husband was much more alert now that the doctor had reduced his morphine!

I think I was justified in thinking the worst was over. The surgeon said he was free of the cancer and he was no longer heavily sedated, so I looked forward to holding his hand and chatting things over, the way we always did. Looking on the positive side, this was a wonderful opportunity for me now to have the role of carer for a change. How desperately I wanted to fulfil the urgency of that role; that need filling every part of me to overflowing. But, how wrong one can be!

As I entered his room, Richard looked at me in a way that I had never experienced before. This person, with whom I had shared everything, was suddenly a stranger. We had already had our fair share of challenges in life, and as far as I was concerned this was just another wave that we would bravely ride. But almost without warning, it didn't seem like *we* any more. We were suddenly two people dealing with not one but two problems. It all felt so wrong – so alien. I wondered if Richard had been given the same information as me. Did he know the cancer was successfully removed and how fortunate it was that he hadn't had keyhole surgery? But clearly, he was as well informed as me. Desperately, desperately wanting to help in some little way, I reached out to make him more comfortable and rearrange his pillows – after all, this was a role that was second nature to me. Sadly, my expertise was in question as Richard irritably suggested that I call for the nurse. I was not, it seemed, even capable of sponging his hands and face; respecting once more his wish to be alone, I quietly left the ward. Tears uncontrollably running down my face, I suddenly understood how Richard had felt some years previous, as I became completely aware of the full impact of my own actions then. Maybe this was some kind of karmic debt, I wondered? But it was now my turn to feel *his* rejection and now that I understood, I also knew how to help.

I never did excuse the nurses for their lack of sensitivity and understanding of my needs as well as their patient's. I had specialized in paediatric nursing so it was second nature to involve those closest to the child in their care. Surely any person with any sensitivity would recognize such a basic need? Unfortunately, there are still qualified nurses who almost claim ownership of *their* patients, undoubtedly fulfilling a need of their own rather than that of the patient they are caring for. It's interesting to note that in many countries in the world, patient care in hospitals is dependent upon family participation and is, indeed, an expectation rather than a choice. I think it's a privilege to be allowed to enter this very special and private space with someone in the hours of their greatest vulnerability. We should indeed feel humbled for the opportunity to fulfil our own purpose of servitude, but at the same time question – whose needs are being met? This last statement may sound somewhat cynical but unless we question in this way, we may well find that it isn't our spiritual growth that benefits, but the reinforcement of our own ego. Everybody feels a sense of inner warmth and satisfaction when they have helped someone in any way. It was the anticipation of that wonderful feeling that seemed to draw me to a career in nursing so many years ago, and I wasn't disappointed. However, I have to question earnestly now what else gave me the drive to leave duty at ten o'clock at night and reappear again at 7 a.m. in the morning? Was it really just my *calling* to help someone during my day, or was there some hidden motive that lay in disguise? I can honestly say that, feeling tired and weary after my shift, I rarely thought about doing anything else. We worked under somewhat harsher conditions than the modern student but perhaps one thing that kept us all focused was the camaraderie amongst fellow students. Without the support we gave to each other, I wonder how many would have dropped out of training. The bond that grew between us was like that of a family; such were the friendships endorsed that I am still in touch with some, forty years later. It's a strange thing to comprehend that the same camaraderie that kept us united and gave us all strength had the potential to throw us into a false sense of security. A nurse's uniform was in itself a symbol of recognition and respect from the outside world. I didn't have to tell anyone that I was a caring, compassionate person who had chosen low pay and long hours in order to fulfil that role, because everyone knew I had. My parents, aunts and uncles were very proud of me, which gave me even more satisfaction, but when I took my uniform off – who was I then?

I was a good and probably 'natural' nurse and I knew that. There was nothing egotistical about me when I was fulfilling my purpose and I believe that's why I did it well. I was so totally committed to the work I was doing that no thoughts, other than those relating to what I was attending to, came into my head – just totally focused. When I came out of nursing, it was not only due to ill health but also to get married. There is no doubt in my mind that getting married softened and perhaps disguised the real reason for me having to give up a role that had become my life, but it also gave me time to reflect and discover exactly what it was that I may have been missing.

It's been difficult listening to the conversations of friends and colleagues as they chewed over their numerous work related problems, even though my own non-involvement was now regarded with some envy by them. I've often yearned to be back in the environment that was so challenging and yet familiar to me, but as the questions that I delved within to answer – I was surprised at my own truth. Did I actually think that I was so important to the profession that they couldn't do without me? No! I had never envisaged any self-importance in my role, but it was contemplation on this question that seemed to trigger the light switch. I was not missing all the aggravation and challenges of the reorganization and changes that my colleagues were enduring. I was missing the role I had played for so many years, leaving me feeling misplaced. I had lost not only something I thought identified me but something – I identified with. I was still a compassionate, caring person, but that was and always will be the nature of who I am. But my own truth had been disguised by the role and my identity with the role that I had played for so long. No wonder I was now feeling an 'outsider'. Never was that feeling more apparent than when illness caused me a complete role reversal. Instead of giving the medicine, I was taking it. Does it matter that we become so attached to a role, and doesn't it make us more effective in that role? Thirty years ago or more I was more than happy to take my identity from the role I was playing, proudly announcing: 'I am a nurse'. As many years later, I have discovered just how much of me has been hiding behind the façade of – *what I was doing*, rather than discovering – *who is my being?*

Compassionate, dedicated and caring though I was, and still remain, I never was a nurse and never could be (any more than the doctor, lawyer or lowly road sweeper, or whatever title is given these days). I was merely acting out a role but – that which I Am – can never be changed. Whatever hat I wear or uniform that adorns me, whatever language I speak portrays no more than the role I attempt to play. I was part of the camaraderie that supported me during my training and that I supported in return. We grew individually stronger through being united, but we were all individuals, all with our own identity; each of us leaving the pack, one by one, to explore outside it – *alone*.

Sadly, we are sometimes surprised when an unlikely person responds to the needs of another. Typically, such a surprise may be delivered through the media when a 'rough' young person (no doubt clad in the obligatory 'hoodie') has spontaneously gone to the aid of an injured old lady or perhaps raised money for the starving in Africa. Why should we be so surprised? Perhaps we are so role orientated that this young person just doesn't fit that role? Any of us who responds to the needs of another, whoever it is, generally acts spontaneously and will be rewarded with an inner feeling that can't be felt by anyone else. We are not, however, fulfilling a role but responding to our true nature, our true identity. Our undivided response to the needs of another makes us an immediate channel for our own divine essence to flow. That very special, almost indescribable inner feeling after the event is our own personal experience of our own Divinity or *Love*. The 'unlikely' young person, now resuming the role of his attire, may well respond to the media and his mates with appropriate pride, but the ego that now conquers his tongue was not that which prompted his compassionate actions. Being a nurse donning the starched white apron and hat before clicking over to the wards made me feel proud too. But no sooner had I heard the cry of a distressed child than my ego-dominated thoughts about the role I was fulfilling abandoned me for the only true connection I would ever have with any of my patients. I was not trying to fulfil the role of my uniform but just allowing the true source of my being to flow naturally and unhindered – for that was my only purpose.

Chapter Sixteen

Richard gave me a card that he had adapted from one of the many 'Get Well' greetings he had received, but this was not a get well card, it was for my birthday. I had not expected him to remember and had nearly forgotten myself until that morning, but it was also a reminder of the month we were in. What was it about April and Easter that had repeatedly made it so eventful for both of us? Both our birthdays are in the glorious month of April and perhaps, for all the reasons we loved it so much and I still do, is that which it represents. April is springtime and spring brings forth new growth, new beginnings and optimism, so maybe it's not a bad time to meet some of those challenges in life, even after illness.

We were all excited about Richard's homecoming. I say all because it seemed that even Meg, Ming and Fred were poised to greet him with wagging tails and contented purrs. It seemed that these days I was always offering encouraging words like, 'won't be long now – be good', and then disappearing for the next five hours, so they probably thought Richard would have more respect for their bladders – all things considered! I certainly wouldn't miss the trips back and forth to the hospital either. People always think it's strange that I was a nurse for such a long time but feel so very uncomfortable in the hospital environment. I don't know whether it relates to some of my earlier, somewhat frightening childhood experiences or to my more recent encounters, but not something I feel high on the agenda to address at this time.

Richard came home with renewed energy and purpose. I say renewed because these were two qualities that were so much a part of him and it was just lovely to see it again. He was bitterly disappointed that he hadn't made it back to China but, thankfully, was ready to raise the white flag graciously in exchange for his health. As if making up for lost time, he engrossed himself in planning our next camping trip to France. He had worked out that if we timed it right, the mandatory three-month ban on lifting would be up just as we were leaving, and then he could at least help with the camping fridge. Both of us were very proud of our so-called 'portable' acquisition and it really added a tone of luxury to our camping experience, though somewhat cheating some may think. I've always been interested in the magical 'no lifting for three months' after abdominal surgery. I wonder if the cut-off point is really that critical since it seems a bit strange that yesterday you couldn't even lift a kettle but, today, you suddenly challenge your body with a camping fridge!

Neither of us was worse for wear and we had a good time as usual, except there was something quite different. We'd been to the same camp site in the Dordogne for quite a few years and this year we had met up with the friends who introduced us to it in the first place. This year, one of our weeks would overlap and they were going to take the pitch next door to us. It was all good fun with barbeques and flowing 'vin rouge' but never before had we been unlucky with the weather. This trip was so different. From the time we arrived to going home, the low oppressive clouds didn't shift. Neither of us said very much about it at the time but as we said goodbye to our friends and headed home, we were unusually pleased to be leaving. During the week we spent with our friends I became increasingly concerned for Peter, for absolutely no apparent reason at all. Part of me put it down to some pretty enthusiastic wine tasting that had gone on the night before, but I felt quite unsettled and told Richard so. We were home, and shortly after their scheduled return Margaret told me that Peter had quite suddenly lost his sight in one eye and was still in hospital in France. It seemed that the expertise of the doctors and the emergency surgery performed saved his sight.

Recovering after an illness of any seriousness always seems to make us want to make up for lost time, indeed, something that I've experienced myself many times. Well Richard certainly intended to fulfil that need, as we would all appreciate – or sometimes, not! It wasn't just making up for lost time that he wanted to do but he seemed to be going through almost a review of his own life. Many people, suddenly awakening to the fragility of life after a life-threatening experience, will change their lifestyle in order to maximize their chances of living at least a bit longer whilst, at the same time, going all out to enjoy what they have. For Richard, it was almost as though his experiences had opened up a whole new understanding of his own vulnerability – which was something he had never chosen to address before. His survival of a life-threatening assault on his body was almost too much for him. There have been times for most of us when we have been the patient recipient of someone's personal recollections, whilst they desperately try to recall every hour of the experience. It seems we are trying to make sense of what may have been a very sudden and dramatic event in our lives, almost like having our own internal counsellor. Richard never mentioned the pain he had suffered or the indignity that I know he'd have felt being in hospital. Whilst wasting no time to get back to normal and start socializing again, almost proud of his own achievement, he took every opportunity to put himself forward as the *cancer survivor*. He knew how fortunate he'd been and now he would try to bring hope to others, almost suggesting: 'If I can do it – so can you'. His sense of humour was back in full swing and everyone affectionately welcomed it.

Chapter Seventeen

Did he know? He certainly didn't let on if he did. It was the Christmas season and the flu season at that. Richard had already had his share but had recovered enough to be Father Christmas for the children's party we were holding for Katy and her friends. Meg was not at all sure about his new role. Seeing an 'intruder' in the dark with a large sack on his back and tapping at the window outside, she did what all good guard dogs should and took a nip at his backside! And whilst all this was going on – 'Mummy Christmas' was inside with the children, who were expectantly and exuberantly wondering if they *really* had heard Prancer, Dancer and Rudolf outside.

The children's party had gone well and now (the weekend before Christmas) it was time to hold what had become a tradition of many years, our own Christmas party. I really did wonder if we should cancel it that year because Richard was still slow to recover from the flu and I was now trying to fight it off. Checking the willingness of each other to go ahead with it, I don't know who was the most stoic, heroic or just plain stubborn. Something inside me said we definitely should and the other part said we shouldn't, so by the time we could discuss it no more, it was too late to cancel. It was now less than an hour before our guests were due to arrive. Both of us having bravely worked throughout the day were now on to the final preparations with me on culinary, Richard on drinks and Katy just proudly running to and fro in her usual eagerness to help and do whatever was asked of her. Whilst Richard keenly awaited the salmon platter to which I had just put the finishing touches, I briefly caught his gaze as he relieved me of the weight, but remember very little thereafter. I recall the hum of voices coming from downstairs as the front door repeatedly opened and closed, my body seemingly burning up with fever and my head belonging somewhere else. I don't know how many flu victims we were responsible for that evening, but it's a memory that few of us would forget for so many reasons.

Friends always regarded our party as a springboard into the festive season. It had become such a tradition over the years that the wonderful quiet and stress free Christmas that always followed would not have seemed quite the same without the 'kick start'. But this Christmas was not normal – in any way. We were all still feeling jaded having not fully recovered from the flu, but there was something about Richard that was really bothering me and I was quite sure it wasn't down to bugs and viruses. Both of us were so sapped of energy that we took it in turns to stay awake and keep Katy company. How awful that Christmas must have been for an eight year old, full of life and fun and who probably felt (in childhood time) that the next Christmas would take forever to come again. How sad was the effect of those experiences on her, when for many years to come she was unable to bear the pain of its memory.

The New Year began with a thud as my deep-seated fear was finally endorsed. We would celebrate the first day of January with Richard being admitted to hospital, but this time I had encouraged him to go to the local hospital where he would be in a ward with the company of other patients. It didn't take very long really, just a quick scan was all that was needed. It was so very sad that they left him guessing for nearly a week – continuously evading his enquiries. Yet again I found myself demanding some answers, even though I was sure I knew what they would be. I found it so difficult watching my beloved best friend, clearly tormented by the sheer lack of information; at the same time, his unwillingness to assert himself whilst seeking the answers intrigued me. This was a man who reserved his gentler, loving side for those closest to him, but was very capable of exhibiting the ruthless and arrogant attributes of a successful businessman when needed. Sometimes perhaps we prolong our ignorance of truth since, once enlightened – it is more difficult for our ears to pretend they didn't hear?

But the truth was delivered. I was fortunately with Richard when the consultant was due to come, but whilst we waited anxiously, he suddenly confronted me with a question of such profundity as to take me completely off my guard. Looking straight into my eyes, he asked –

"What do you think he will say, Sue?"

I knew what the consultant would say, but how was I to tell him? But as compassion filled my heart – the words were out.

"I think he will tell you the cancer is back," I said, fighting back the tears.

"Hmm – I wonder how long I have?"

I didn't have to say any more. The door opened and the consultant introduced himself. He was a consultant *Oncologist*. That word was just ringing in my ears – as I too knew that I could escape the truth no longer.

It took five minutes, or possibly ten. Thank goodness I told him, I thought, as the doctor made an assumption that Richard knew his own diagnosis and somewhat dispassionately announced that treatment was only palliative. Equally devastating was his answer to Richard's further enquiry when he was told that he had a maximum of six months to live. I wonder if we live up to those predictions of life expectancy or is medicine really so advanced that, whilst unable to offer hope, it can tell us when our time on earth is up? Richard wanted to know and I have always respected his bravery for asking, and indeed his need to know.

He stayed in hospital that night, giving us both space to assimilate the events of the day. How do you keep such information from an eight year old, and do we have the right to deny a child access to something that is going to affect the rest of their life? How much of our hesitancy is due to preservation of our own feelings? It seems there will always be questions unanswered and maybe some regrets, but we were both determined that *guilt* was a word that would have no meaning – for either of us.

We talked, we laughed and we cried together – hour after hour, day after day. There was nothing that was left unsaid. These were the most precious days of our lives but instead of waiting for them to end, we would live and experience every single moment, as it arrived. We never looked at tomorrow or even the next hour, we just learnt to inhale and treasure the moment we were in because that is all any of us can share – *this moment*.

How very honoured I was to be so privileged to have shared Richard's very last months, days, hours and finally, minutes. Shortly after helping him up the stairs to bed and preparing to keep vigil over him, he quietly directed me –

"Go to sleep now, darling; you're keeping me awake."

And so he left – *six months* to the week. No longer was it Richard, my husband, lover and best friend lying beside me. He had taken leave of his body, but feeling his arms around me, I *knew* – not of his loved ones.

Chapter Eighteen

If I had a pound for every time a bereaved woman or man has shrugged their shoulders and wryly said to me something like: 'Well yes, you have to get by, don't you' – as if there was no choice, I'd be rich now. It is delivered as a statement of fact but more often than not it's a subtle enquiry, just in case anyone else has found another way. The belief that life has very little to offer when a partner dies or a treasured relationship comes to an end saddens me greatly. Such a belief is almost disrespectful of the relationship, suggestive that the beautiful growth within it was only of value for its duration. In any relationship, as it grows, so do the people in it, but the relationship itself has grown as a result of two people working together for what must be a common goal. Over the years, it is seen that the two people are now working almost as one and experiencing a magical union, otherwise known as *harmony*. It's no wonder then that the partner left behind, like the bereaving swan that has lost its mate, believes that part of him or her *self* – is missing.

Bereavement is an emotion that every one of us will experience at some time during our lives – some, more than others. For some the bereaving process seems to go on forever, as does the accompanying suffering. Psychologists seem largely to share the hypothesis that it is a process that is not complete until each stage has been experienced. I am not a psychologist and don't have a professional right to my opinion, but I question the true nature of this emotion – if in fact, it is one at all? Ask ten people in the street what bereavement means and they will all probably mention the word *death*. Some may qualify this as being a *meaningful* death to the bereaved; we don't usually suffer this process following the death of someone we don't know or care about, although we may feel sympathy and sadness.

Many words are used to try and describe the pain of our grief in an attempt to try and make sense of our own suffering: emptiness, sadness, despair, depression, loneliness and hopelessness are all frequently used vocabulary to somehow express our deepest feelings of loss. Friends and experts will tell us to hold on tight and let our grief slowly lose its grip. After the many times I have personally experienced that place, I probably would have been the first to agree. At the time it seems impossible to rush it or accelerate the process, but to patiently wait for the sun to finally brighten up those dark grey days.

I wonder why we consider bereavement only to be attached to death? We seem to understand that it doesn't have to be human loss that creates it, many of us having felt the pain of losing our dog, cat or other pet. So is the suffering of bereavement merely an unavoidable human condition that we must go through? Is it just another name for the pain we feel when we lose a loved one? Maybe the answer is not straightforward and my own thoughts on it have been greatly constrained when I am reminded that it isn't solely a human condition at all. Many animals, notably elephants, whales, dolphins, monkeys and canines demonstrate all the evidence of the grieving process when an infant or close member of the group dies. Perhaps other animals experience the same grief but don't demonstrate it in a recognizable way to us humans? Maybe the animal kingdom has a more sophisticated way of dealing with it; or maybe, the mourning process is not in itself an emotion at all – but the thoughts that create the onward waves of suffering? If *thought* is a major part of bereavement – shouldn't we question some of our beliefs about the non-thinking animal kingdom? Maybe we would discover that the presumed hierarchical structure of our planet may not be quite as we believe?

Different cultures, ethnicities and religions all have their own way of grieving. The symbolic or noisy expressions that are frequently exhibited as part of a ritual that all the mourners are familiar with seems mysteriously to have a sudden cut-off time, after which life returns to normal. Does it really return to normal? Can we be trained to know when to respectfully adjust our thoughts in order to do so? In the West, we are accustomed to taking our time and if time doesn't work for us, a doctor can always help out with some antidepressants – suggestive itself that we're suffering from an illness. In the more organized and ritualistic forms of bereavement, life has to go on or otherwise claim more lives. These people don't usually have the privilege to take their time as we do. Like the grieving elephant or dolphin, they know they are the only ones who can stop their own suffering and that life won't wait for them to feel better. In order to survive, they must move forward and resume where they, very temporarily, left off.

And that is what we too need to remember. The death of a loved one is probably (to most of us) our greatest experience of human suffering, at the time. I say 'at the time' because, as with all suffering, the pain passes eventually and if we know what is causing the pain, we are halfway there. Nothing can bring our loved one back – so why don't we accept that simple fact? We all know that death means departure and physical separation. Our pain is enhanced by not only our refusal to accept our loss, but our failure to understand *why* we won't accept it. Bereavement may be the cause of our greatest human suffering, but within its experience is the greatest gift of spiritual growth. When we realize that our ongoing suffering is not something that life has handed out to us, we also begin to understand that we prefer the comfort of feeling the pain because it feels more secure to us than moving into unknown territory. We can't change our mindset because life has become one string of attachments, and our attachment to our loved one is unimaginably difficult to break.

We believe that attachment is a measure of our love, so to 'let go' makes us feel so uncomfortable with our own emotions that we find ourselves having to choose between the pain of attachment and the pain of letting go. Change doesn't happen unless we really want it to and are prepared to play our part in bringing it about. It's no good *wishing* you could lose weight, get a job, or give up smoking if you don't make the first move; after which – help is at your door.

I have always been an independent person and perceived by many as a so-called 'fighter', but my own personal growth had greatly benefited from the union I had with my partner. Richard, always acknowledging the strengths I brought to the relationship, had the comforting reassurance of my ability to cope when he was no longer here. But doesn't the word *cope* really mean – *get by*? 'Getting by' surely indicates – getting through life. We are not here to get through it, we are here to live it – to *be* it. Whatever events that have passed are precious foundations of our future, but like the passing chapters of our book – each contributing to the main event. We are somehow dishonouring a relationship by just surviving on its memories alone rather than putting its teachings to use in the next chapter of our lives.

We don't all have fond memories of a relationship that we've been in but it's important to remember that we learn and grow – because of it, even if we don't whilst we are in it. I believe now that every event in our lives truly is a gift by which to learn, but if we are not open to its teachings the gift is wasted. If two people are not working towards the same goal (even if they think they are), there never can be harmony within the union; there never can actually be a union within that relationship and it's better to recognize that, than hope it's just going to change. However, the potential for learning and personal growth from this dysfunctional relationship makes it every bit as valuable as the relationship deemed *good* – providing we are willing to accept the lessons it offers. Many so-called 'happy partnerships' thrive on the unquestioning servitude of one of its members but whilst each partner may be content to accept the 'conditions' of the relationship, the opportunity for growth is stifled by its own stagnancy.

Is the feeling of loss, when something so good is taken away from us, greater than the feelings of relief – when something so painful has ceased? How many times have I asked myself that question and yet still fail to find the answer? My loss was very, very great, but my fear whilst anticipating that loss was even greater. I couldn't imagine what it would be like without Richard. It was a bit like the inevitability of a baby's birth when the mother has been carrying it for nine months, and yet seemingly finds it unbelievable that birth, like death – is inescapable. I was never in denial about his prognosis, but it never felt completely real and was more like being in a dream. I used to look at the upturned lips of his wistful smile whilst he embarrassed friends, joking about his departure. His apparent vitality made part of me wonder if there could possibly be a mistake and yet, the other part of me knew that wasn't the case. In retrospect, as I look at some of the photographs taken at that time, I can't believe that I could ever have doubted it for a moment. How interesting it is that so often we believe what our minds want us to believe, not what truth is telling us.

Waiting for a loved one to die is a waiting experience like no other. Whilst Richard was clinging to every second of life and planning long-term holidays in the hopes that he could cheat the hand of his destiny, I became more and more exhausted trying to keep up. For him, every new plan was proof that he was alive, but for me, it heightened the pain and the anticipation of an experience totally unknown to me. Sometimes I would silently scream within – almost demanding to know when the pain would end for us all and then feel great pangs of guilt in case I hastened the process by asking. I'd had the misfortune to have lost most of the elders in my family, and Katy had been to more funerals in her young years than most adults attend in a lifetime. The grieving process is something that no one can prepare us for since the experience will never be the same for any two of us. But neither will any two experiences be the same for any one individual. For me, I believe that process took place over the preceding six months when the profundity of the questions asked began to quietly prepare me for what was to come.

For many years it seemed – I had been *waiting*. As most young women of my era, I hoped one day to fall in love and have a family, but it seemed it wasn't to be. One relationship after another was disappointing and unfulfilling, leading me to finally believe that, that which I was seeking was unobtainable. But later, the lure of foreign travel was also the journey to fulfilment of my dream, inaccessible before perhaps because I was yet to be on the right road, at the right time. If life has shown me but one certainty, it is to know – there *is* a plan for all of us. How we achieve it depends on looking out for the subtle changes when one road may appear – the same as the other.

Those beautiful eleven years were but the briefest interlude in my life. It had been a lonely road until I was joined by a dear friend to share my journey, but sadly, all too soon, as the path divided – we would have to say goodbye. I watched him as he quietly steeled himself away, wishing… that we could have journeyed just a little longer, together. But I still had a way to go and work to do. This I knew was now my path to tread – *alone*.

Chapter Nineteen

He had to go so I could grow. Why did those words resound so clearly within me? No one could ever say our relationship had retarded my growth. On the contrary, I had always been independent and yet learnt to put my trust in others; I had learnt to receive as well as give; I had learnt to acknowledge my own achievements and my own contributions to life. How much I had grown in those golden years, but I knew – the bird was yet upon the wing. The work I came to do, the journey I came to take had still a way to travel.

None of us can ever remember the details of what, I believe, may have been a kind of pre-earthly covenant, even if we share that belief. Maybe within my own quest was a need to make sense of being gifted with the experience of total fulfilment, only to have it snatched away in what seemed like a flash? To remind ourselves of the nature of all relationships is to acknowledge that they must either grow or they will wilt and die; those that remain static are not relationships at all, but just a state of inertness. The growth of a relationship itself depends on the willingness of those within it to allow the other the freedom to grow – which is the real test of human union and thus partnership.

There was always respect for each other's freedom to develop personally as well as within our union, but I always knew that the ultimate challenge of our relationship was still on hold. Richard had demonstrated an unspoken acknowledgment of my healing abilities many times when he had introduced me to people he seemed to know I could help. His confidence in me may have followed the sudden disappearance of a long-standing unsightly lump that he had on his forehead. Sadly, it wasn't until his last months that he shocked me by openly acknowledging my gift, but by that time it was too late to integrate it into something our relationship could share. Although I had always been truthful about my spiritual beliefs, I was never prepared to risk the two things in my life that were so precious to me by pursuing what was, clearly, sensitive terrain for both of us. I was so fortunate that the path we both shared was never threatened by my own spiritual journey and as eager as I was to 'get on with it', there was always an inner knowing that there was no hurry. I was already on my path – as he was on his.

Richard never left. I don't know how he managed it but the temporary spiritual absence that leaves one totally bereft after a loved one's passing never happened. When my eight year old daughter told me, "Daddy was down in the goat's house with me" or that, "Daddy has just come through the wall" – I suppose I wasn't too surprised. What never fails to amaze me though is the innocence and ease with which children accept their spiritual sightings. They are still so in tune with things outside this worldly existence of ours that it's all very normal for them. For me, it was just a wonderful confirmation that Richard truly was very near, as indeed he had hoped might be the case – should my comforting beliefs turn out to be true.

I can see my life so far divided into what looks like a map. As I scan over it, the parts of the map that I have explored are defined by a line of demarcation like the boundary lines of a county, but each one adjoining to each other at its borders. I can see there is much of the terrain I have yet to travel and am reminded of the gifts of each excursion, the difficulties overcome and the joy of overcoming them. But I am also reminded that the distance I travel has no bearing on the richness of my journey.

Chapter Twenty

When I am at the end of my life, I will almost certainly view the last twenty-five years as having the highest mountains and most rugged paths, but the most beautiful views are seen from the highest vantage point, making the frequently hard toil so very worthwhile.

Where would I begin? I would give back to life some of the goodness life has bestowed on me. I had an opportunity to love and help children, animals and people. It was as though I were being fed with energy direct from the 'power station' and before long, our little animal family had become a menagerie, both inside and out. We fostered dogs, rabbits and cats, and those we didn't think would find a home too soon we just took into the fold. Bleating kid goats and quacking ducks completed the farmyard and Meg, our Border collie, was delighted to find she had work to do again keeping her own pack of six rescued dogs in line. They were all of varying breeds and temperament, so as well as trying to decide if she was in charge of the ducks *and* the goats as well (before it became obvious) she had her work cut out for her. Every time Katy came home from school she would do a quick head count to see who else had joined the family, but she was in tune with the animals as sensitively as with her father.

Animals are great healers and to be around them and care for them is indeed a gift and a privilege to mankind. I only wish we would appreciate the part that animals can play in our world and then, maybe, we would love and respect them for their pure devotional friendship with which they reward us. When Richard died, Meg immediately assumed a hyper-protective role, not only of her fast growing family but, more significantly, Katy and me. Her protectiveness caused me some concerns at times when

I had to remind her who the pack leader was, but she was quick to learn and her willingness to stay focused and alert for her beloved 'charges' was touching – almost surreal.

Responding to RSPCA requests to foster more rabbits, puppies or kittens was only part of my new role, when – 'the lady with a farmyard in her garden' suddenly began to be offered sick and injured animals at her door as well. There was always a cage or box standing by to receive a rescued bird, hedgehog, or whatever else people would find on their walks! The word *sudden* is not used inappropriately or with any exaggeration and, as my mind recalls the occasion, I am moved in wonderment yet again. Not only does there seem to be a divine plan that sets our path, but also a reminder of our direction. That reminder to get us back on track is often a painful one; at other times, it seems frankly *miraculous*!

Few people knew of my healing abilities since I always believed that it was not my role to actively look for patients. I was probably right, but unfortunately my gift was something that I was reluctant to talk about openly; almost as though it would make people wary of me. How few years ago it was when the last mystic was killed, through fear? Yes, thankfully we have moved on since then (particularly in the last two or three decades), but anything that cannot be either proven or seen is still a problem to the sceptics – until otherwise experienced. I had a phone call one day from a good friend of mine. Good friends usually know quite a lot about each other, but this wasn't the case at the time. Cathy's friendship had shown its true colours when she allowed me the space to unload my emotions, both before and after Richard's death. I will never forget the foundations of what went on to become a much-valued friendship. Perhaps most memorable was when (completely out of the blue) she asked me if I could help their pet rabbit? I was speechless. Perhaps the strangest thing was that Cathy didn't seem to know herself why she had come to me, let alone know that I was a healer.

Getting in my car, I soon arrived at my friend's house, not wanting to distress the little rabbit unnecessarily by moving him. That visit was to be repeated many times over in the next two weeks or so. The poor rabbit (only a few months old) had a horrible abscess on his face that so many of these creatures suffer from. The vet had already been treating it for some time before finally having to admit defeat suggesting, 'the only real option' for little Whisper. I have long realized that (as is usually the case) I was the last resort, but I didn't mind that because I also knew – his only chance.

As I took the struggling little creature from my friend, my hands were tingling and burning more profoundly than I had ever experienced before – like sparks of energy. I wondered if I could keep him still for long enough to focus that energy, but I needn't have worried then or thereafter for any animal. The little chap relaxed into my lap and went to sleep until I withdrew my hands. My experience and knowledge of pet rabbits has shown me what vulnerable creatures they are. It's hardly surprising that Mother Nature designed them to be so fertile, but why they are ever suggested as low maintenance and perfect pets for children I will never know. I've had more broken hearts over rabbits than any other pet.

Little Whisper quickly responded to the healing channelled into his tiny face and this much-loved rabbit went on to live a record number of years, before finally scampering the meadows of his spiritual dwelling. My friend and her family, now sharing my truth, would soon be helping me to share it with others who needed it. Within a week or so of helping Whisper I was invited by a friend to attend a demonstration of clairvoyance. I'd been to these evenings before, but if past experiences were anything to go by it seemed unlikely that any of my many loved ones in spirit could brave such a public event. And so my thoughts were confirmed as Geraldine Whitney (the medium) finally prepared to 'close down' – leaving me strangely disappointed, but not for long. Announcing that this was to be her very last message, she looked at me whilst giving me amazing evidence of Richard's survival. But I remember little else, other than to recall the words that came through her lips –

"Take your light from under the bushel now!"

The following day, I took another phone call. Could I "help a friend dying from cancer?"

I didn't have to worry about telling people that I was a healer after that because there was no need – as if by divine assistance, the word just got round. My diary filling up, I was finally fulfilling my real purpose. Throughout my life I have repeatedly felt the guidance from a source I can only describe as – *intangible* and yet – *accessible*. All of us have access to this guidance and the source from whence it comes. It is constantly with us, not out there somewhere – right *here*. The more we consciously acknowledge it and let ourselves be engulfed into its serenity and peace, the more skilled we become to receive and use the divine power that it is.

The more one seeks spiritual truth, the more we realize how much more there is to reveal and how little we seem to know. And yet, we also begin to understand that there is nothing to learn, except the skills to remove the veil of deception that has enshrouded our truth for so long. None of us is blessed with any greater spiritual content than anyone else, but some are more aware of the essence of their own being than others. People sometimes ask me about my own healing abilities and sometimes (almost enviably) express a wish that they could do likewise. And they could – if they really wanted to. It isn't a *wish* that makes us a healer (or anything else come to that), it's the absolute and pure *intention* to want to effect change. In this case – another's suffering. The purity of that intention is divine energy in itself, but most of us just *wish* we could help rather than listening to our own source speaking to us. Geraldine (now a friend of mine) tells the story of how she was running a workshop for a group of people, when one of the students was suddenly overcome with a migraine headache. Clearly, the group was very sympathetic but, quite suddenly, a flash of light darted from one of the students straight over to the migraine sufferer. The woman, from whom the light had originated, informed my friend that she desperately wanted to take the pain away for her fellow student. *That* – is healing; *that* is intention. I have questioned my own healing abilities on many occasions, not only trying to understand it but, at times, believing I should be experiencing the energy flow with some sort of textbook accuracy. In truth, I never have been sensitive to seeing or feeling energy in the way some describe it. My hands seem to have an intuition all of their own and I just allow them the freedom to be guided accordingly – even though I may have no idea of the strategy. I don't try to understand it any more but just accept and give thanks for it. I am open to whatever guidance is offered me but I also trust that a much greater power than the body I stand in knows where and when that guidance is needed. The primary and most essential part of being a healer is to *want* to help someone above all else. After that, the only obstacle preventing us from channelling and delivering the healing energy is the power of our own *ego*. It is our ego in the form of thought that tells us 'we can't do it' or 'we may fail'. It is our own ego that interrupts the flow by its constant need for self-gratification and control. The tightrope walker keeps perfect balance by focusing his complete attention on the present moment of his task. The awareness of where he is *now* leaves no space for doubts and 'what ifs'. As soon as he brings his awareness on to the dangers below him, his balance is lost and his ego has engulfed his intention. Thinking we can do it takes us only as far as the high wire. *Knowing* we can do it – takes us safely across.

I am reminded of one of the many wonderful stories told us by Miss Moore, our elderly nurse tutor, during my training forty years ago. Whilst working as a midwife during the war, the building she was in was on fire after an air raid. With no other choice other than to remain still and accept her fate, she was forced to cross some sort of temporary bridge several floors up over to the adjacent building, in order to take the babies in her care across to safety. She related with such gracious modesty how, being acknowledged for her bravery after the event, she was taken to see quite what she had achieved. She promptly fainted! The story was supposed to demonstrate the role of adrenalin in our fright, fight, flight mechanism, but perhaps of greater significance was her intention and thus focus beyond all thought – to get herself and her babies to safety. Nothing can be achieved without intention, which is also the fundamental quality of all healers wherever they are. Many would call this wonderful piece of heroism an act of 'mind over matter' but this is a phrase often used to explain something we feel is really not explanatory. Such acts of heroism are not the result of mind over matter but – being over mind; something quite different.

Chapter Twenty-One

I, like most people I suppose, have tried to 'beat the system' by challenging that inner voice with what my mind was dictating and the ego demanding. The 'New Age' trend to think positively rather than negatively about our desires and aspirations seems a reasonable enough recommendation. After all, if we really want something, it seems counterproductive to believe that we are not going to get it. Unfortunately, when we're dissatisfied with life, we may well test the power of positive thinking to achieve our goals, but then wonder – why we are still unhappy or discontented?

The self-help and so-called *spiritual* shelves of any bookshop are full of books telling us how to create and mould our own lives. The book you are reading at the moment (although relating a personal journey) does so with the intention to help others on their journey. Unfortunately, along with positive thinking, it seems evident from many of these books that there is a current philosophy that believes we can have anything we want in life and furthermore – we haven't done it *right* if we don't get what we want. All we have to do to get it is to see no barriers and think positively. Perhaps I am sounding a bit cynical but that – I am not. Life has taught me that we don't always get what we believe we want, but we do receive that which we need. There is a subtle difference between these two words which unfortunately we are apt to ignore. There is a wise saying that warns: 'Be careful what you wish for.'

As one who has experienced the power of positive thinking first hand, I also have to say that I have experienced its negative side as well. Positive thinking is like a prayer and when we pray, we must be sure that what we ask for is necessarily good for us.

Prayer is an amazingly powerful creative energy and so is positive thinking; indeed, we have seen in parts of the world the negative and devastating effects of using this gift erroneously. But the negative side of positive thinking or prayer isn't necessarily the result of misuse of such power; it can happen quite unintentionally. When we are solely intent or passionate about something we want to achieve, we become so focused on getting it that we fail to notice the signposts directing us up an alternative route.

My desire to help others in the past has been so intense as to become overbearing for me. It is the meaning of this word that is so appropriate here. Someone who we describe as 'overbearing' suppresses us in favour of their own voice, thoughts, or personality and this is exactly what we allow our own minds to do, not to someone else but ourselves. I had still to learn that whilst I could channel healing energy to someone, I was not responsible for their healing, but all the time I allowed my mind to overpower me I would believe otherwise. Life offers us many choices and we will frequently make decisions that we may later regret as part of the learning and growing process. Although we may be uncomfortable with our choice, it won't be a wasted experience and we can never expect to get it right all the time. However, we will continue to head in the wrong direction as long as our only driving force is our mind. If we just plunge in, randomly making choices in our lives in accordance to whatever may be in vogue at the time, we would be no more than robots. But allowing our heads to take over *is* robotic since we completely ignore the guidance of our own *divinity, higher self or spiritual centre* and march on regardless, as though it wasn't there. In effect, we become brainwashed by our own ego. When we start to make demands, regardless of our inner voice or intuition, we will cause ourselves unnecessary suffering – as I did.

I had always loved children. Even as a child myself I can remember wanting to love and protect them, almost as though it was a perfectly natural instinct, which of course it was. When I embarked on a nursing career I knew paediatrics would be my choice of specialty. I didn't have to fight for it or spend hours of deliberation, even though I had started my career as a general trained nurse. Everything just flowed and there could not be any doubt which path I should take. I didn't even have to make the first move because the paediatricians had recommended me for secondment to do my children's training. I just knew that I was heading in the right direction. And so, my path flourished, opening out into new and inviting tributaries that flowed into yet another seemingly 'designed' course of advancement, before I was finally responsible for training paediatric nurses myself. Even then, I knew any choice I made would be the right one for me – for the time being anyway.

Having resigned myself that love and marriage was not going to happen for me, almost unconsciously I found myself dreaming and scheming of ways I could help deprived children, without having a partner. My thoughts flicked from one continent to another as I questioned where the greatest need lay. I remember so well the excitement I felt inside me as I just knew that this was something I could really do. I still hadn't decided in my mind whether I should go to another part of the world or offer children in my own country love and a home. When it comes to childhood deprivation and suffering – can we ever make a choice between the child who is starving and sick, and the child who is perhaps poorly parented or abused? These questions were being tossed over and over in my mind at the time and, sadly, I seem to have moved on very little in finding any answers. I perhaps should have questioned my own indecisiveness but, fortunately, I was spared the pain of soul searching.

By some quirk of destiny or fate, I was not going to give my life to the children of Africa or Asia in the way I was planning. My marriage and problems with my health diverted my good intentions but did not make me forget them. Not long after Richard's death I was reminded of the plan that he and I were researching, when we'd hoped to help young teenage girls who, for one reason or another, had lost their parental and family ties. In the light of his sad diagnosis those intentions had to be abandoned as well, but the flame would soon be rekindled by an advertisement I saw in the local paper.

The local authority was desperately trying to attract prospective families who could adopt one of the many children in their care, and they were having an informative evening for interested families. My instinctive hesitation at first was overridden by a pleading daughter, now aged eleven. To be able to share our home and extend our family for such a worthwhile cause was irresistible. Having raised all the relative arguments with Katy to check she understood the reality of what she would be sharing and surrendering – not for a week or month but for life, I was as content as I could be with her response. She seemed to be amazingly informed about the whole thing, having clearly thought things over herself already. However, I didn't need to be a psychic to know that neither of us could fully appreciate the way our lives would change, until we reached a time of no return.

My own dearest wish, to give another child the same chance in life that Katy was privileged to have, was my most powerful driving force towards achievement of that goal, even though right from the start I had niggling reservations. I was snapped up by the adoption authority as a potential adoptive parent. Katy impressed them with her mature and well-informed approach to adoption and I was apparently equally impressive with my broad and varied background with children.

So the process had started and would take over a year to complete. On a frequent and regular basis we were asked to build up our own personal profile, which included both sensitive and emotional betrayal at times. I understood the necessity for such intrusion and was only too happy to provide the evidence of both my parental and Katy's sisterly abilities. The many animals of our household were also frequently praised by us for the gentle, loving nature they demonstrated when meeting the numerous children they had already interacted with.

As time went on, our anticipation of the enormous changes we were preparing for demanded a frequent reality check. Clearly, adoption of any child is not going to be easy, but the parents who agree to take on that role must be ready to love and treat that child every bit as much as their own child. It is the stability of the family unit that the new addition is seeking and, yet, they themselves could threaten that stability as soon as they step over the threshold. I was preparing to make a commitment that was going to change three people's lives forever, and I could not be sure in which way. Richard was no longer here to enter the debate or to discuss tirelessly all the avenues for consideration, as we so frequently did when we were seeking answers. But the guidance was coming – if I would only recognize it.

I wanted to tick the boxes as we went. I knew the adoption department were keen to recommend us but I also knew that, before we could be approved by the panel, I would need to provide medical evidence of my ongoing good health. It always seemed to me more appropriate to have that particular box ticked in the early stages, thus saving any unnecessary disap-pointment or, indeed, sparing public resources. I had been told that my medical condition and the medication was no less acceptable than a person with insulin dependent diabetes. Providing my health issues were stable and not expected to change dramatically, there was no foreseeable problem. I already knew I had the backing of my own doctors, so why was I repeatedly feeling so uneasy – even as a possible child was being matched with us?

And so the day finally arrived. Our profiles were being presented to the adoption panel who would decide on our suitability to become an adoptive family. I had been told by the adoption team we had been working with for over a year that I should have no worries. It was just before Christmas and Katy made it quite clear that approval from the panel would be her best Christmas present ever. Rushing in from school that evening to see if there was any news, she could hardly contain her excitement. I could hardly fight the tears back when the phone finally rang and our shocked social worker told me – what I already knew. We had been rejected.

Chapter Twenty-Two

Although it was thought we had all the necessary qualities of an adoptive family and my medical condition was stable, there was concern about its unpredictability. I was angry. We were both angry for so many reasons, least of all – how did these people think I was caring for the family I already had? We were both angry because a deserving child had been denied a loving home and new chance in life. I was angry with myself because, inwardly, I knew I had taken the wrong road. I knew that I would look back thankfully, rather than with regret. I couldn't help regret though, because I was the adult who was supposed to be protecting my own child and my desire to help another had almost jeopardized her happiness – long term.

It is through life experience and the way we use and interpret that experience that help us to formulate opinions and make decisions that will further affect our lives. Without being exposed to life, we may get through it, but will always lack the real tools to help us live in it. Any parent knows that the fine balance between giving a child the freedom to explore their own potential but, at the same time, protecting them physically and mentally can be quite daunting. Anyone who has had the privilege of working with children knows that every one of them is an individual, bringing with them something quite special, unique. As adults, we assume the role of teacher, protector, and guide, but I believe we are often blind to the real purpose of that relationship – when the children themselves become *our* most valued teacher.

My inability to sometimes remember that Katy was still a child was because, from her earliest years, she had a knowing aura about her that almost belied her young age. When our concept of a child is challenged by our own experience of that young person, it is difficult to remind ourselves of the role that experience plays in their own learning process. Until the challenges of life test the true progress of our journey, how are we to know how well equipped we are to face the rest of it? As I've said before, when two people walk the road together, only the soul who treads his foot – can feel the terrain beneath him.

The love of my youth was to walk the fells and just soak up the beautiful views and the tranquil essence of the surrounding countryside: the carpet of purple heather, the sound of bleating sheep contentedly munching their way through the bracken, until nervously scurrying away when realizing I was not of their kind. The beautiful autumnal colours just fed my soul, but many are the times when I have not been alone on these trips and had company to enjoy them with. As anyone who shares a deep passion with another knows the presence of a common empathy is the essential ingredient for a growing bond. It's so delightful to share such an experience and yet is something that has provoked a discreet but powerful enquiry within me, that I remember struggling with even as a child. When you and I stand at the top of the mountain and look across at the beautiful view – do you see what I see? Do you feel what I feel? Why am I so transfixed, hesitant to move away from the magnificent vista that now seems to embody me – whilst you may smile and head back down the track? What do we actually share in this life? Are we on an even lonelier journey than we previously believed?

This feeling of *aloneness*, rather than *loneliness*, is something that has followed me all my days and yet, as I stand on the outside looking in, there has always been a shadow there beside me. There has always been a *silent witness* in perfect harmony with my being, allowing me the freedom of my own expression. I have heard much said about soulmates and their special place in our romantic union, but I believe we are reunited with that special person at any time and in any relationship during our lives. I was a shy five year old when I first became aware of that beautiful spiritual harmony that is inexplicably re-awoken when reunion with a soulmate takes place. I knew that John and I had always been together and even though I would see him rarely as a child, I knew he was both a healer and a seer. I don't know how I knew these things because not only did I not have a language to describe it, it was certainly not spoken about in the family until many years later. Although I would have met him when I was considerably younger, my earliest recollection, marked by the magic of the moment, was when he gave me a beautiful doll that his mother (also a seer) had made. As I took the doll, promising to look after such a precious gift, I knew I was also being given something intangible. I was totally at one with this lovely man, and *his* gift seemed to become my gift. We were soulmates on earth until the day he died; always my friend, healer, teacher, and guide, but the essence of our bond will stay with me, forever.

Soulmates seem to be reunited at different times in our lives according to our need and, perhaps, the spiritual covenant of two souls. The relationship with my uncle was one that always seemed a bit one-sided. His was the gift to give, all the time. As the receiver I was on constant alert to find any way I could to balance the order of our relationship, but it wasn't until much later in his life when I understood that dealing with his own discomfort to receive was part of *his* spiritual journey. When John died, I was married with five year old Katy. He knew and I knew that his time was very near. Just a few days before, we quietly acknowledged that I wouldn't see him again. The telephone rang and I heard the shaky voice of his elderly wife. I dreaded hearing her words as she related how he'd just gone to stoke the boiler, then suddenly left this world – within minutes. John stole away as silently and modestly as he had lived his life. His earthly duty now fulfilled, he left us with his final message. Both my sister Geraldine and I (coming from different parts of the country) arrived at the crematorium in the fog – just as his funeral service had finished.

John had touched so many people's lives that there would clearly be a big gap to fill, but that in itself was all part of the learning process. Believing that life goes on beyond the grave is very different to *knowing* that it does. Our faith and trust is sorely tested when we lose one who has been so close to us, but we must still give ourselves permission to grieve from the physical plane and understand our need to heal. Our spiritual expression through a physical existence is all part of our earthly experience, so why should we try to deny ourselves the indulgence to grieve, through the medium of our own temporary state?

As I have already said, soulmates seem to come into our lives at preordained times, but unlike many other relationships we have in life, it is a union of unconditional love on both sides. Sometimes a soulmate relationship is experienced between two siblings or, perhaps, parent and child. I believe, before taking a physical body, we choose the parents who will provide us with the best opportunities for our spiritual growth, but that feels very different to the intangible connection between soulmates that may, or may not, be related. We recognize our soulmate almost instantly and yet we can't say how, or why. We feel immediately safe with this person, who may otherwise be a total stranger and we always seem to know – this was no chance meeting.

When your own child is also your soulmate, perhaps the process of recognition is quite different from one who is not so directly related to you. Except when we have more than one child, we are not able to compare relationships, so we are left with what we *know* to be the truth within us. I believe the child soulmate is not just a close relationship we share with that son or daughter. I've been blessed with two or three very close friends who have always 'been there' for me (as I for them) ever since our first meeting. But these dear friends who would do anything for me and have been beside me for considerable parts of my journey – I know – are not my soulmates. These are people who are very important in my life and at the same time very precious to me. These are people with whom I can share my innermost feelings, but they are not my soulmates with whom my soul and theirs instantly recognizes some inner connection beyond our deepest friendship and love.

I feel so blessed in life to have the relationship with my daughter who, I have no doubt, is not only my soulmate but seemingly – my *twin soul*. As she walks her path, quite different and yet parallel to mine, it seems we are reminded of our true covenant and our true connection that yet we can't quite recall. My interest in the spiritual connections between people is something of an ongoing quest of mine but as with any other evidence of spiritual truth, verification can be offered only from the *source* of that – whose evidence we seek.

Chapter Twenty-Three

We had never gone for the option of fostering children as I'd already acknowledged my difficulties with fostering animals. The process was so painful watching the prettiest puppies being chosen in favour of the less attractive ones, just desperate to get themselves noticed by the prospective new owners. As a result, my little family was getting bigger and bigger. That wasn't what was likely to happen if we fostered children but I didn't feel it fair on Katy to have the uncertainty of transient family members at that time in her life.

It's strange how things can change. Suddenly we were being offered the opportunity to foster, even though we were refused adoption. I could understand that in the event of me being ill, it was probably less traumatic to move a child who was with us temporarily anyway than to uproot a youngster who had just been given her 'dream family'. At first we were reluctant, but when we recalled the reasons for taking a child into our home in the first place, it became obvious that there was no difference in adoption or fostering, or so we thought. The placement matching for age and sex would stay the same and we would not take children under five because I didn't feel it was safe for them with a pond in the garden and so many animals. Katy had specifically asked that we would only take girls and the top age of the child would be ten years.

I don't know if one can be any more prepared for the unpredictable outcome of fostering a child, any more than we can be for our own children. We are all so individual and we all react differently to our upbringing and environment. Our genes are so variable that even the temperaments and characters of siblings react quite differently to the environment they are brought up in.

Our experience of life and our responses to it are unique. When we bring our own children up, although there are sometimes disappointments and also some surprises, we can usually expect them to reflect the values consistent with the environment in which they were raised. Hopefully, we would not wish for anything more than a *reflection*; we are not looking to produce a clone of ourselves but a self-reliant and valuable member of society who has his or her own destiny to fulfil, not ours, or what we may choose for them. A lot of us say that our only wish for our children is for them to be happy. I have often shared these thoughts for my own daughter, but being happy is just what it says – being. We don't find it out there in money, jobs, careers or anything that is 'outside us'. Some people say, more accurately maybe, that happiness is a state of mind. However, in order for the mind to be in that state, it must be receptive to the source of happiness which is, I prefer to believe – our natural state of being. Thinkers and philosophers have pondered over the nature of happiness for hundreds of years, and yet we are still asking the same questions today – 'What is happiness and what makes us happy?' Many of us spend much of our lives alternating between an apparent state of happiness and one of unhappiness or even indifference. But there are others who sadly believe they have never experienced happiness in their lives and others who, even with limited material assets – seem to be in that constant state of bliss.

Pondering on such a reflection, we could be justified in thinking that relinquishing our materialistic lives in favour perhaps of one of monastic living would reward us with the happiness we seek. What we always seem to overlook is that rarely is a life of such humble existence chosen to *find* happiness, but because one is aware of the true nature of their happiness and of that which destroys it. I don't feel inclined to become a nun but over the years I have realized that happiness is not just another emotion.

It is my personal experience of the expression of my own spiritual essence, as it joyfully celebrates our harmonious accord within the *oneness* of my *being*. This is the nature of true happiness, within us all.

I have been trying to recall the reason I wanted to adopt or subsequently foster children. I could come up with many reasons, but the all-encompassing one was my belief that I could make these children happy. My failure to do that was to leave a lot of unhappiness at more than one doorstep. I could spend my life blaming social services for misplacing the children we took and would be totally justified in doing so. None of the placement criteria previously agreed upon, including age and gender, was respected. The first child to come to us became very violent and had to leave us as suddenly as he came. For someone who had worked so closely with children for most of my working life, I was totally unprepared and shaken by his unpredictable behaviour, but was persuaded to take another child. When I heard that we were being sent a two year old my heart sank as I thought about the difficulties of keeping him safe with six dogs, five cats and a pond to fall in! I needn't have worried because he was a delightful little tuffy, striding confidently through the dogs – most of which being taller than him. Having witnessed the injuries and grief following dog bites, I am exceedingly respectful of the dangers. You can never be overconfident about a dog's predictability because, sadly, we can't be sure of the child's either. In this case, our pack, headed by Meg, clearly sensed the vulnerability of this little chap from the start and seemed to miss him as much as we did when he returned home.

Having had such a traumatic first placement really knocked my confidence, but that's not all it did. I had been told that I was this particular child's last chance to have a long-term home, if not a permanent one. It's regrettable that some of the relevant history was kept from me but it was good to know that my capabilities had been respected, even if I'd failed to live up to their expectations. There were no surprises for me at first. I had worked before with children, damaged by their traumatic or deprived backgrounds, and this little lad was no different. It isn't possible and indeed would not be helpful to discuss the intricacies of this placement; but when so suddenly and unpleasantly it came to an end, I couldn't stop asking myself – where had I gone wrong?

When one day we were asked to take two children we had to hastily reassess our sleeping accommodation, which was hardly sufficient for another child. We took in two eight year old brothers who, like many children in foster care, had a long history of numerous placements. Like all the other children, they made an instant connection with the animals which was immediately reciprocated by the dogs, cats and goats. I was amazed and relieved to see the respect these youngsters showed them, as a major concern of mine abated, for a while anyway. I have always believed that a true connection with animals (as with all of nature) is one that also connects us with our own *essence*. There is something very special about a relationship of such mutual respect and understanding, our only true communication being dependent upon something we can experience – but not name.

Children are in many ways so similar to animals and have very similar needs. We need to protect them and care for them and as with any animal, children will trust until life teaches them otherwise. In the case of our thousands of children in care the lesson sadly comes, more often, from personal experience. Learning to be a foster carer was also learnt by personal experience. Although common issues and problems were outlined to me, there was nothing that could have prepared me for the role I had now accepted. I knew that both children were in conflict with each other and yet, like any siblings, had an unbreakable bond when feeling threatened. It doesn't take very much for a child who has lived their life in uncertainty to feel threatened; something they will almost self-induce by pushing harder and harder at the boundaries. My understanding of these children, I began to realize, was negligible, and although I was quick to learn, it was never going to be fast enough to safeguard my own family and animals, let alone help the children.

I've always had a belief (that some may perceive as naïve) that anything to do with human behaviour and relationships can be solved by love. It was naïve in many respects but I still believe the power of love knocks down many barriers and forms many foundations. To my surprise, our placement officer had commented several times 'how readily I invested in the children in my care'. I was puzzled by her comment, believing that my investment in these children was a necessity if I was going to help change their lives, and I always took it as a criticism. It wasn't until much later when I began to understand what she meant.

I have never found it difficult to give and never found it hard to love, but neither did I know that there were times when you could give too much, too quickly. There were many problems and issues to be worked through but no more than one would expect given the nature of the boys' history. We jelled pretty well at first and the tolerant nature of both myself and Katy was an attribute that would supposedly help us all to build a solid and hopefully long-lasting relationship.

Once the initial honeymoon period was over and the boundaries stretched to breaking point, I discovered that the boys were taking their frustration and confusion out on the only ones they had securely bonded with, almost with the intent to destroy what little they had. Discovering that they had taken to taunting the animals was heartbreaking but it taught me much about myself as well. I learnt for the first time that my love *did* have boundaries and sometimes did come with conditions; Katy was one and the animals were the other. It was that insight that made me realize that fostering children was not my destiny and never would be. It took me a long time to come to terms with the fact that I hadn't failed. It took me even longer to understand that although it wasn't my destiny or my purpose to be a foster carer, the process by which I'd made that discovery would help me to accomplish what I really am here for.

I spent many hours internalizing the events of the previous couple of years and my reactions to them. It was difficult for me to separate the guilt I was feeling for failing the children and my personal sense of failure. I had thankfully raised the white flag before the animals had suffered unduly or shown any adverse reactions to their experience, but I had no idea of the impact it might have had on Katy and to this day am still wondering, since she claims to have no recollection of that period at all. Both of us had bonded sufficiently with at least one of these children for there to be few days when we didn't allow our thoughts to wonder too – what yet another traumatic placement had meant for them? Unfortunately, as we learnt to our sadness, that was a question that would never be answered. Once out of our care it wasn't our privilege to know or even for the children to know – we still love them.

I can understand why Katy can't recall these events because, for me, it's as though I was taken somewhere else and brought back again. It had all seemed such a terrible waste of time and energy that I found it difficult to comprehend how my good intentions could have gone so wrong. I had repeatedly been told that two of the placements we had taken were some of the most difficult, but that didn't make me feel any better about myself.

It was my *coming back* that finally cleared the clouded vision that had prevented me from seeing. It definitely hadn't been a waste of time or energy but I was yet to value its worth. It wasn't only the children who pushed all the boundaries, hell bent on destroying what they had – I did too. Right from the start I was repeatedly given all the signals and intuition that perhaps this wasn't for me, but my ego wouldn't let go. Every time I let him sleep for a while, the message would get stronger. It was made so easy for me to decline when the panel rejected me but that just made me more determined; the *power of positive thinking* had become a weapon, rather than a tool.

As we've said before... there are many routes to choose from and some get there sooner than others. I'm not sure I would have consciously chosen this particular one, but that's where our trust comes in, doesn't it. If I had trusted my inner voice rather than *thinking* I knew better, I may have saved a lot of heartache, but a power much greater than me was overseeing my journey; a power that knew another way to teach me the same lesson. I never seem to make a straight run of things and, like the boys, could almost be accused of self-destruction at times. However, I invariably come out, thankful and much richer for the experience. I wish I could say the same for the children but I suspect their experiences in life have taught them another way. We can never see the benefits of what we may call negative experiences at the time and yet, we are all given the gift to turn negative to positive.

My own feelings of failure to be the perfect parental replacement for these children had left many painful questions in my mind unanswered. I suppose it's only natural under such circum-stances to compare ourselves with those we are, truthfully, trying to emulate. Many, many people have said to me throughout the course of my life how much they would have loved to have trained as a nurse. Others would have liked to have the working relationship I had with sick or injured animals, but both admirers were quick to realize that something prevented them from doing that. At the time, I would feel puzzled or annoyed, knowing that I too had to learn to toughen up in order to respond to the needs of either sick humans or animals. It wasn't until much later that I recognized that these people *knew* their limitations. It isn't merely our desire to do something, essential though it is, that ensures our fulfilment of that role, but something that inspires us beyond the realms of thought. It is not the destiny of us all to walk the same path, fulfil the same dreams or enjoy the same health or wealth. We may excuse our deficiencies and shortcomings because we don't receive the same natural attributes, but we must learn to harness that which we are given and exploit it to its greatest potential. Too many of us could have been spared the pain of our misinterpretation if we'd have been more receptive to the still small voice of our own being. Only too often, the ego is off on another power trip that is bound to lead us up the wrong road.

It was not my destiny to help children in the way I had thought. I was already effectively helping them in many other ways, both practically and financially, but my mind was thirsty for gratification – yes, it was me who was seeking something for me and I had only just acknowledged it. I could love these children, have fun with them and provide them with a safe environment, but it wasn't enough. That is what I wanted, but it wasn't what they needed. I had misguidedly believed that love was the basis of all our communication – it was, but the love I was offering was unrecognizable to them. I was not prepared for the boundaries that were forced, or equipped to deal with them when they were crossed. Everything I was doing was counterproductive. My expectation that these children would trust me because I *knew* they could now seems so naïve. Trust takes a long time to establish but the process of getting there was not within my gift.

Whilst my compassion fed my desire to help, my desire was feeding my ego. Our egos are so very persuasive at times that we are in danger of succumbing to their somewhat devious nature. The *inner voice* is very different from the 'voice in our head'.

Chapter Twenty-Four

Those past couple of years of my life seemed to have floated in and out like a dream, and a bad one at that. I replay that dream sometimes but the more I watch it, the more and more detached I become from it, wondering if I was ever really in it. Richard had now been gone for five years, even though it still felt like yesterday. I still expected him to call me just before coming home from work; still thought I could hear his car coming up the drive and even fifteen years on, I wanted to pick up the phone to tell him bits of news that I believed I could share with him. I wondered what he'd have to say about our adventures since he'd been gone. How much easier it would have been with the strength of his energy around, I often thought. I had rarely sat down to have a good cry or got angry with him for going – or God, for taking him. I had believed that my independence and self-sufficiency meant I wasn't experiencing bereavement in the way that was expected of me and got quite irritated when people seemed to think they could predict whatever stage I was supposed to be *at*. I didn't need anyone to say, 'It's ok to cry,' I knew it was, but that's not what I wanted to do, at least – not until I had unlocked the space to do so. It would be a very sad world if we had no appreciation of others' needs, but our insistence on believing that we know what they are is quite puzzling. Not one of us shares the same journey or has the same experience and we are all so very individual in the way we perceive that journey. I just needed someone to give me a safe space when I wanted to talk, and to let me be when I couldn't.

Katy and I had entered a different mode of bereavement after the boys left. I think it was as much associated with what we had lost and now recovered, rather than what we'd hoped for but failed to attain. I remember feeling numb and empty and found the need to open all the windows, as if to change the energy. One of the boys was a first class escape artist who tested the boundaries in the truest sense; when he finally got bored of scaling the fences, he thought he would climb out of the top floor window! I don't know what it was about this particular child but his apparent lack of fear was something that I admired and perhaps envied; not because I wanted to conquer my fear of heights but because he had learnt to *rise* above it – pardon the pun! At what point should society step in and offer children a home where they will at least have an equal chance of discovering who they are? Surely we owe it to them and to society itself to save them from drowning whilst they are still paddling – not taking their last breath out at sea? I often believe if we had been fostering just the one child, as initially planned, he might still be living with us. Did I let him down or was that part of his journey too? Do they think of us as many times as I think of them... wondering where they are now?

Katy and I were sitting on the rocks watching the dolphins play out at sea, whilst eating the best fish and chips I'd ever tasted. We too had decided the best thing to do was escape for a while, and had taken our little caravan to Wales for the week. When we take ourselves away from all that is familiar and soak up the vast and beautiful energy of all that is not of man's making, nature saturates our inner being with her healing presence. Mesmerized by these beautiful creatures (as they skilfully played 'dodgems' with the rolling surf) was itself profoundly healing.

Chapter Twenty-Five

How do you condense ten years into a few pages? The past two years had left a legacy that was not so apparent at the time, but was yet to demonstrate its effect on my body. Silently, my worst enemy had yet again been creeping in, as if in some mean feat, bursting to prove a point. The stress that I believed myself to be immune from had finally won over my body, which was demanding more and more cortisone to keep it ticking over. What does one say when trying to relate such a period of your life? I am still trying to recall the sequence of events and the process myself, so how can I tell anyone else about it?

I was having a major exacerbation of an illness that I believed to be safely under control with the medication that I had now been taking for many years. That was until I realized that I had been misdiagnosed and wrongly treated for the previous ten years. As I have said before, I don't want this very significant time in my life to become an opportunity to blame because that isn't the purpose of my writing. I think it's fair to say that many errors of judgment which hampered diagnostic conclusions also, in their turn, contributed greatly to my own personal suffering.

Part of the reason why I think it unhelpful to scrutinize every step of my medical history, apart from the difficulties in recalling all the data, is that it would detract from the teachings of this particularly difficult and yet beautiful time in my life. We all believe we know what our own needs are in order to live life happily and comfortably. It is those needs which become our greatest driving force as we seek to satisfy even the most basic ones. When we are hungry we seek food; thirsty, we seek water; when we are in pain, we seek to rid ourselves of our discomfort.

Pain is a word with such a variable meaning to us all that, once again, we discover how difficult it is to appreciate the pain of another. Our only means of perceiving another's pain must be through our own experience and that, more often than not, is the measure we use. Anyone who has been in hospital with a painful condition will invariably recall being asked to assess their pain on a scale of one to ten. That kind of assessment is clearly needed to establish the progress of the condition in accordance to the patient's own perception, but it tells us little else. My pain is not your pain, so how can you ever truly know what I feel, or I know what you feel? When we hear the word pain we generally have a thought of something that hurts or a physical discomfort, but when we really examine our use of the word, we begin to realize what a much broader meaning it has and how inappropriately it is sometimes used and inadequately interpreted. Physical pain is a natural reaction to injury of any description and is nature's way of telling us that something is wrong and to remove ourselves from danger. The beautiful nervous pathway from the point of injury through to the brain and back allows us to quickly retract our hand from the hot kettle or fire without even thinking about it. Sadly we are not always spared the consequential injury from the accident, but that natural reflex continues; however impossible it is, we will continue to try and rid ourselves – no longer of the offending cause, but the pain itself. And here begins the lesson.

Any animal will try and escape from pain as part of its survival mechanism, but an animal having escaped the cause of the pain will react very differently to their subsequent discomfort. The healing process comes instinctively to them and they seem to accept the situation they are in and act accordingly, even if it is to lie down quietly and die. Most humans are quite different and do what we do best – *fight*. We speak emotionally of those amongst us *fighting* cancer or finally losing their *battle* with a terminal disease. I am not being disrespectful or glib about such a sensitive issue and am certainly not trying to degrade the bravery and frequently stoical attitude to their suffering. But it is the word 'suffer' that has become one of such significance to me on my own journey as have I also *battled* to rid myself of the pain I carried.

When we fail to acknowledge or indeed even know the cause of our pain, the thing that we focus on most of all is the pain itself. That's not too difficult to appreciate since it's that which is apparently causing our discomfort, so we invest all our energy into ridding ourselves of it. We will of course never be free of the pain until we have first identified its cause, but in our oblivion – we keep trying anyway. How many of us have watched a young child trying to carry out a simple task whilst he becomes increasingly frustrated due to his inability to appreciate the fundamental sequence of the operation? His frustration leads to tears and more frustration as he suffers pitifully, unable to identify the problem or the cause and thus the solution.

Our pain, frequently called suffering, is not even the direct cause of our suffering, and yet our suffering can so readily be experienced as pain. Although the two words are very akin and we seem to accept that they are interchangeable, the recognition of the subtle difference between them opens the door to a much greater understanding of our own difficulties in life. Both pain and suffering occur at varying levels in life and we are most fortunate if we manage to escape either; whilst others seem to endure more than their fair share. Mindful of the suffering of others, I have many times questioned the role of my own suffering in relationship to my life and my spiritual evolvement. But, as many times that I have embraced the teachings of the so-called negative experiences, I have finally understood their sole purpose as being *my soul* purpose. Our minds, in their incessant search for answers, grasp egotistically to the concept of suffering as being essential to our own understanding of others. How ill-informed we are. We don't have to suffer the pain to be compassionate, but our own suffering and pain offers itself as a portal to our own spiritual truth. Having finally surrendered to its invitation, our eyes are opened more widely than ever before and we see for the first time not only the cause of our own suffering but that of all humanity.

Chapter Twenty-Six

I had been doing so well for several years that even with the occasional setback I had never envisaged returning to my precortisone days. I can see now that something was wrong when I required increasingly higher doses in order to maintain my energy levels, but was horribly shocked when things started going very wrong. With a review of my diagnosis it seemed that the long drawn-out process of hospital appointments, tests, investigations and hospitalization was to begin yet again. But this time, there was no Richard to hold the fort and remind me of what I *did* have rather than what I didn't. This time it was all up to Katy. I wondered if she shared with me my feelings of *déjà vu*. Here she was in her early teens at a time when life was throwing her her own challenges and, at the same time, fast becoming carer to me. We still had six dogs to be walked and all the other animals to be cared for but as hard as it became, I think they kept us going. I just can't imagine a house without animals now.

Maybe it was more gradual than I now recall because with skilful planning I was still able to do most of the essential tasks in the house. Although my energy and muscle power could be dramatically cut off without warning, I got used to maximizing the first two or three hours of energy I had in the morning before finally submitting. These were the *good* times before things got really difficult. During these times I was still offering a healing service both at home and in the hospice; the strange thing being that I never actually had to refuse anyone. Even when my body was most debilitated, just as people had started arriving again when I was a bit stronger, the phone almost mysteriously stopped ringing when I was too weak to work. Some mornings when I was going to the hospice I prayed for the strength to get me there, but until being forced to take a break, I always did get there and it wasn't only the patients that benefited. As soon as I became focused in my work I received the strength to carry on, becoming magically energized beyond all comprehension. The many anxious moments poor Katy had endured on my behalf, whilst I insisted on honouring my commitments, were once again unfounded.

There is almost a common belief that young people not only should be but are – free from the many worries that may come their way in their more mature years. In many respects, I suppose this parental expectation is often tinted with a little envy of their children's apparent freedom. When we bring our children into the world, we only ever see ourselves as their carers, protectors and teachers but when the role is reversed, it can be more painful than the cause of the reversal. Katy had not only lost her father but was now witnessing a rapid deterioration in her mother. Her spontaneous anticipation of not only my physical but also my psychological needs was touching. Her sensitivity to show her appreciation of my maternal role (that I myself so sadly felt was failing her) was probably more precious to me than the more practical role she now fulfilled. But as she bravely soldiered on, stoically and silently in denial of all her fears, my daughter emerged not only my soulmate, but my very best friend. Not only was she my tower of strength but my sole purpose to survive – the continuous taunting that life was offering me.

I always think *offer* is a lovely word. It suggests an opportunity without obligation; a freedom of choice to perhaps take it or leave it. The phrase *freedom of choice* must be one of the most exploited in recent years. Isn't that what we would all like for ourselves, wherever we are in the world? Surely it's a philosophy based on basic human rights and needs and yet, so many in the world are seemingly denied that privilege. To open a debate on such a vast question is perhaps beyond the scope of my writing. We don't all have the same experiences in life, and some of the experiences we do have leave us very little scope of choice at all. Someone who is caught up in torrential floods may have the choice of remaining where he is and risk drowning or clinging precariously to a piece of driftwood with the slightly better odds that he could survive. I have questioned many times if we can really consider this sort of dilemma as presenting any choice at all? However, the choice this person eventually takes may determine whether he lives or dies so yes – he did have a choice. Sometimes our choices in life are limited to either accepting something that we can't change or cause our self still more pain and suffering by fighting it, in the belief that we can. If our choice results in showing us that we made the wrong one (more frequently referred to as a mistake), we may live to regret it. Poor choices can completely change the route of our journey, but indulgence in our regrets is yet another poor choice that will destroy the rest of it.

Mention the word *spiritual* and some people, having made a quick assumption about you, will discreetly move away. There are so many people now using this word as though they themselves have just invented it that I'm not surprised some of us are confused about its meaning. Books and workshops seem to offer the ultimate spiritual guidance on anything from 'angel power' to finding our own personal guide. I have done my fair share of reading during my spiritual quest and I have to say – most of the books I have read have just made themselves known to me. When I look back now on my somewhat varied collection, I wonder what on earth attracted me to certain material and yet, each assisted to take me to the next step, each has played its part (however briefly) on my long process of introspection. I seem to have moved on a long way since then. The bookstores have also moved on a long way as well. When I first started researching material there was but a small shelf, hidden away in the corner of the local bookstore. I can remember edging my way over, as others did, hoping to browse unobtrusively whilst feeling as though I were looking at a seedy magazine. Paying for the book at the counter was no less painful, as I discreetly turned it over so people behind me in the queue couldn't see what I was purchasing. But yes, we have moved on and now the entire top floor of that bookstore is devoted to self-help and the 'spiritual seeker' and you'd have a hard time pretending you were heading for the poetry or cookery section now! How wonderful that the world seems to be waking up to the part of us we've tried to keep locked up and disguised for so long.

As I've discovered, there is no book, no teacher or even spiritual master that can do it for us, but they can point the way to the next signpost and facilitate the process. We may believe that life is a spiritual journey but that belief remains without verification until we seek to explore that belief. To understand something is knowledge, but knowledge of any kind is quite worthless unless we exploit it to expand our understanding of its significance in the larger picture. Thousands of years ago we believed our planet to be flat, until it was discovered that not only was it a suspended sphere but part of a whole galaxy of planets. We may be brilliant at maths and achieve the highest grades to prove it, but unless we use it, it becomes a useless piece of information that idles somewhere in our brain, unable to grow due to the limitations of its separateness. We don't have to become a scientist because we've studied chemistry, but knowledge is the foundation to all wisdom. Limited knowledge leads to limitation in our views and actions, and causes a false sense of isolation and separation. Discord and wars come from limitation of knowledge and yet we see throughout the world how ignorance is nurtured – as the most powerful weapon of mass control.

We strive to give our children the best education in order for them to succeed in the world, but how many of us perceive *success* as an imaginary package of a career, good lifestyle and wealth? When will we start to teach our children the real values in life and show them – they are not the job they do; the lifestyle they have; the clothes they wear? The answer is so simple – when we know this truth ourselves. When we learn that we are not our thoughts and our minds; when we know we are not our job or our lifestyle; then will our children know it and their children's children know it. So it could be said that we have a duty to our children and to society to never stop seeking truth. If we are in a delusional state ourselves we will continue to breed delusion. We can't be expected to access something we don't even know exists, but we need to stay open and vigilant to all possibilities and remove the word *never* from our vocabulary. Perhaps the greatest gift to man would be the wisdom that comes from knowing truth. Truth is within us all and attainable to us all. The gift of truth, however, is neither mine nor anyone else's to give; it cannot be shared between friends or lovers, between religious teachers or humble seekers. We cannot progress on our own path by clinging obliviously to the paths of others. We know the truth of others when it resonates with the deepest part of our selves but as we accept it as our own, we must be alert to its transitory nature, as we broaden the spectrum of our true awareness.

Chapter Twenty-Seven

I had spent many hours compassionately holding the hands of both men and women suffering with cancer, sometimes as they approached their final hours in this life. It was a humbling and privileged experience to be invited to share the most sacred part of their journey. The time spent with these people, in the hospice or their own homes, taught me so much about healing and endorsed my own beliefs about the interconnection between us all. Pain and suffering so often seems to reveal this connection as, once again, we observe its humble exposure during our greatest vulnerability in sickness, war, famine, floods or indeed any crisis that will always demonstrate our collective connection through our collective compassion – *collective Love*. No wonder people feel so bereft when the crisis is over and the camaraderie wanes.

The miracle of healing works in so many wondrous ways, knowing no boundaries. There doesn't have to be someone acting on our behalf as the channel of its magnificent energy. We are all channels of healing, both for ourselves and for others. So often, we either forget our own gift to heal or lose touch with it for a while by allowing our own channel to become blocked and stagnant. A practising healer can become blocked and ineffective purely by allowing themselves to connect with their thoughts, rather than the clarity of their intention. Healing is the transmission of pure *love* delivered from our purest intention; if we have to think about what we are giving, we effectively hand over to an impostor.

The expectations of healing are difficult to predict for a new recipient since the experience can vary dramatically from one person to another, and from one healing to another. I believe this fascinating variation is an indication of the way our body uses the healing energy in accordance to its needs at the time. Although most people find it a peaceful and relaxing experience, many are unaware of its wider benefits until maybe they are on their way home or even later. Sometime after Richard died, I needed some urgent help for a back problem for which traditional medicine was giving me little relief. Unused to scouring the free local newspaper, for some reason I hesitated before throwing it away as usual. However, glancing through it disinterestedly, I stumbled upon a healing group just a short distance from where I lived. When I arrived I was instantly unenthused and was both agitated and annoyed to discover that this 'drop-in centre' seemed to be more of a lunchtime social group than a healing centre. I watched with some interest, but also disdain, as people chattered around me whilst eating their sandwiches apparently awaiting their turn. Even the healers were holding chatty conversations whilst they worked, but this was neither the experience I had expected nor the way I conducted my own healing sessions. My unyielding belief on how things should be done left little room for acceptance – thus my equally unyielding judgment. Shuffling in my seat as I prepared to leave, having decided the lack of privacy and background chatter was not for me, I was beckoned to move into the 'healing circle'. Somewhat reluctantly, due more to embarrassment than optimism, I hobbled over to take my turn. I will never forget that day as long as I live. I felt nothing – absolutely nothing – by way of any healing energy that may be touching me, past the compassion of the healers. I made my donation and gave my thanks, still hobbling out the door, sadly disappointed. But not for long! After painfully getting into my car and starting to drive home, something lifted within me, revealing a buoyancy and joy that I'd forgotten was missing. A deep depression that I hadn't even been aware of, yet had lingered within since Richard's death, had clearly taken leave of me. My back problems didn't disappear quite so dramatically, but after weeks of acute pain, the twenty-four hour delay after my visit was magical. By accident I had seemingly found this group of people, but the real way and purpose I had been guided to them – was almost beyond my belief.

My own work as a healer has long taught me that we must trust the essence and direction of that healing because a far greater power than me supervises its flow. Having *trust* means – literally handing over and putting our faith usually in someone or something other than ourselves. I have been asked as many times as I have asked of myself: 'What is it that we are expected to invest our complete trust in?' Many people resist the possibility that there may be a *higher power* that we can entrust, believing only in their own earthly efforts. To a large extent I go along with those thoughts. Without our own effort – nothing worthwhile in life is achieved but unfortunately, there are many occasions when attainment of our goals needs a little extra back room assistance to make it achievable. Most of us have experienced an inner *knowing* about something that we cannot quite elicit and, yet, acknowledge the experience as one beyond the realms of our own understanding. When we are very young, we place implicit trust in our parents and, sadly only too often, anybody who resembles them. That impeccable trust will continue until something shakes its foundations, after which nothing can be quite the same again.

One of my earliest memories that caused me to question the faith I put in others was when I was very young and in hospital. Having to be cajoled into quiet cooperation to accept the more than unpleasant treatments I was receiving, one particular nurse bribed me with all sorts of prizes, on a regular basis. The let-down was that they never arrived, despite her writing notes on the back of her apron to remind herself.

We have all experienced things that shake our trust in people. How difficult is it then for us to put our trust into something we cannot see? What is it that makes even the non-believer break into prayer when quite suddenly and dramatically either their life or the life of someone close to them is at risk? Why do we continuously choose to lock out – even deny the only part of us that is resistant to all that is not of its own nature and remains constant and everlasting? Do we not answer our own searching questions just by asking them? Are we just too afraid to allow our intellect to acknowledge something that we have to admit… is beyond our rational comprehension?

These are some of the many questions that I have asked on my journey, but never was I so determined to have them answered as when my health began to fail my physical body. As I struggled week after week to honour my commitment at the hospice, it was an opportunity for me to forget for a while my own tremulous journey, whilst I allowed others to share with me theirs. The more I listened to the words being spoken, the greater was my understanding of their meaning, but it was more than under-standing – it was absolute empathy. At first, I found this total empathy with these people very disturbing, particularly in view of many of their prognoses. I don't know why but I used to spend my drive home not just questioning my feelings, but almost trying to rid myself of them. It was quite some time before the 'light went on', but when it did – it was like coming out of the darkness of my cave. I was in tune with the fear these people held in their hearts but as I got to know them well, I knew it wasn't a fear of death or even necessarily of dying. It was a fear of losing one's life; a fear of not fulfilling hopes and dreams; a fear of leaving loved ones and children before they had even reached maturity; a fear of wondering how they would be without you; a fear of dependency; a fear of what it was doing to those you were dependent upon. And the greatest fear of all – the fear of facing their fears. The curtain lifted and the light came in, as I saw for the first time my own mirror image in the people who were now my friends. I didn't need to be sick to learn what I had that day, but it seemed it may have been the only messenger I would respond to, and that was just the easy part.

Chapter Twenty-Eight

As they quietly left their temporary lodgings and returned to their spiritual home, I sadly had to say goodbye to many of the friends I had shared so much with at the hospice. But now it was also my time to leave, not to my spiritual home but on to the next part of my journey. I had received all the promptings on many occasions but, unwilling to listen, my body had finally given me no choice. I was frequently too fatigued to put food in my mouth. The stairs I had to climb to go to bed became a physical challenge that finally surpassed the capabilities of the body I had always been able to cajole to go just that little bit further. I now know that my attitude towards this beautiful creation was nothing short of abusive. I felt like the abandoned owner of a clapped-out car; tweaked up at the garage so many times until there was finally no more to be done to keep it on the road.

Loneliness, aloneness – how can two words sound so similar and yet have such different meanings? I have never been lonely, and although I sympathize and can understand loneliness, it is something for which I hope never to be tested. Thankfully, I've always enjoyed my own company and frequently seek it in order to be with my own thoughts, away from the distraction of others. That isn't to say that I'm a recluse or disengage from others' company; there is nobody who enjoys more an evening amongst friends and like-minded people, but I am always pleased to come back to the place I feel most comfortable.

My increasing ill health and disability presented me with a feeling of aloneness that I hadn't experienced before. This wasn't the wonderful self-imposed experience of being alone when I revelled quietly and spontaneously into my own creativity. This was aloneness that was cruelly forced upon me by my suffering and inability to operate normally; my growing feelings of separation becoming a focus of my suffering in itself. All the while I was able to persuade my body to reach a certain level of achievement, I was happy to accept its difficulties as a mere challenge. But finally, being faced with complete loss of control was probably the greatest factor of my increasing isolation and, yet, also the greatest driving force behind my spiritual quest. Before my illness, which until now had been controlled or masked for ten years, I was rarely to be found quietly engaged in passive mode. Even when I courteously allowed my body a short reprieve to take sustenance, the mind that controlled it was never at rest. How many meals, I wonder, have I prepared in haste and then eaten without even experiencing the taste or texture on my tongue, my thoughts ever engaged in my next pursuit? How could I have regarded the beautiful sustenance of life with little more respect than the fuel that runs my car?

If only I knew then what I know now – how many times has that thought taunted me. But it troubles me no longer because I am now at peace with its teachings. It seems there are lessons even in the process of trying to understand another lesson. As already seen, some of us seem to be very resilient to life's lessons and, at times, willing to test their reality with almost a stoic defiance. Others find it difficult to grasp the lesson contained within the experience at all, thus subjecting ourselves to more pain and more suffering next time. As a sick children's nurse I used to find it heartbreaking to watch the unnecessary suffering of these little ones. It was impossible to convince them how much of the pain they experienced during a procedure was due to their resistance to the treatment, rather than the treatment itself. What a simple lesson to learn we may think, and yet most of us are still on the road that teaches us just that.

My father had somehow instilled in me as a child the need to 'brave the pain' and not to make a fuss about nothing. In fact, my father was a strong healthy chap in those days and perhaps saw any weaknesses in his children's health as a personal failure. The need to be strong lest I showed my weaknesses was something that has had some adverse effects, least of all attributing to my own feelings of failure. I recall only too well sitting in the art class (my favourite lesson) in my new school. My head was throbbing with pain and my body felt as though it was on fire, but the fear and embarrassment of asking if I could go home overrode my desperation to do so. When later the doctor said he thought I had meningitis I knew I must be quite ill, but the greatest hurt and confusion of all was being chastised for not telling someone I was ill!

I believe this need to show that I was tough was not innate but something that was taught me. Usually in the process of learning, we seek to understand the lesson. Even the child who is abused will attempt to discover what part of his behaviour evokes the reactions of his abuser, but I just never questioned. I loved my father dearly and, although recognizing some of his own difficulties, I admired what I believed to be his strength of character. I didn't want to let him or myself down, but as much as I would like to convince myself otherwise, I know that the real underlying reason was my fear. It's difficult to perceive how one can fear their father's wrath when I can never recall him ever physically punishing either my sister or myself, although that wasn't the case for my brother. I have often thought about the fear I felt in those childhood days and wish I had the opportunity to change it by challenging the truth of the message my father gave me. He was a lovely man and my love for him will never wane. However, his message that sickness was a sign of weakness severely hampered not only the diagnostic process, but my ability to accept my own increasing disability as I tried relentlessly to prove my strength, if not to others, to myself.

Again I am reminded of the harsh lessons of inherited ignorance and the cruelness of its deception. Acceptance of our own disabilities isn't necessarily a reflection of our childhood upbringing, but it does reflect the way we perceive ourselves and how we believe others perceive us.

Chapter Twenty-Nine

Once a problem has occurred, whether it was our own fault or not, we can't do anything about that which has happened. If we spill the milk we can mop it up; break a leg and we can get it mended; but there is nothing we can do to turn the clock back and neither can we prevent some of the events that may occur as a result of that incident. We may have spilt the last pint of milk we had in the fridge; we may not be able to drive because we injured a leg; we may have our whole life turned round because we are sick. We cannot do anything about these situations either but sadly, we never believe that and rapidly become one of the most frequent causes of our own human suffering – when our thoughts believe they are at the helm.

When chronic illness started to creep up on me, the smile on my face still reflected my eternal hope and optimism. The unpredictable nature of the physical process, whilst frustrating, had at least allowed me to continue my hospice work. Knowing that I could still give and I could still play my part and fulfil that yearning which was instinctive within me was so necessary for my own psyche. I was maintaining some sort of normality and my ability to help others probably made me still feel needed and of some value. This *need to be needed* was quietly creeping into my consciousness as something that I 'needed' to address – but not yet.

I didn't look too much at what was happening to me in those days, and I could only focus on a magic cure that would come from an equally magical diagnosis. I believed wholeheartedly that just knowing what was happening in my body was the key to my own self-healing. Learning that my body had turned upon itself and become its own enemy was a lot to take in. I felt as though my own private army had turned against me and I couldn't stop them. How very disloyal. Why would my own defences let me down? I felt as though I was in a scene from *Doctor Who* when the crazy Daleks just mow anything down in their path. Thankfully, I wasn't given a life-threatening diagnosis but certainly a life challenging one, and even the variation of opinions on that caused frustration and anguish. There was no magic medication, treatment or therapy; there was not even a pathology that the more scientific part of my mind could apply itself to in order to make sense of it. My body had simply seen itself as its own enemy. What greater statement can you make? But who *really* was the enemy? That was the question that never left me, never gave me any peace, until one day I received my answer – but not in the way I had perhaps anticipated.

As one who lives her life now in quiet acceptance of some physical restrictions, I am reminded of the lessons given so that I might find this place. It wasn't the physical restrictions that I needed to learn about because there was little I could do to change the course of events. As I lay on the settee one day finally unable to deny the 'call of nature' any more, I tried repeatedly to raise my body and get up to go to the bathroom. I was in agonizing pain and my muscles too weak to respond to my demands. It was one time too many that my body had refused to cooperate, and I had finally seen what a physical mess I was in. The most frightening thing of all was the realization that I was not in control any longer and there was nowhere to go – except where I was taken. I looked at the scenario before me in total disbelief and suppressed anger, as if I had been cruelly cheated out of what was rightfully mine. All the hopes and ambitions as yet still unfulfilled stood like raw boulders of rock awaiting the stonemason's chisel, but the stonemason had gone away. My potential was now put to rest – wasted. And like the rock, bare to the elements, I was stripped to the rawness of my *being* with nothing between me and that which I am – totally exposed. There was no longer a place to hide; with nothing to lose, I suddenly expressed my anger and frustration, crying out for help to an invisible audience. There have been a few profound spiritual experiences in my life, but this was one that would give me the key to the rest of it, when my thoughts became still and I heard with such clarity the words – *'Let Go.'*

I would like to tell you that I leapt off the settee, threw away my stick and jumped for joy, a cured woman. But none of those things happened. In fact, I think I probably forgot that I needed to get up. I was almost too frightened to move in case the words, that already I was questioning as a dream yet still resounding in my head, might lose their power. This message wasn't one that would help me fight my battle of illness. These were the words that would lead me to the knowledge that there was no battle to fight, let alone win – except within my own mind. This was just the beginning, but now I had the key and could open the door, just as soon as I was ready.

Chapter Thirty

To want to take your own life is a desperate action to avoid the pain of living. It's an action that leaves those left behind feeling bereft, guilty and angry at the same time. I remember only too well when one of our closest friends took his own life, just months before Richard's life was taken from him. To this day, the questions are unanswered. Why such a talented, lovely and seemingly level-headed and contented chap would do such a thing? Seeing the waste of a precious life that was probably less than halfway to its completion was quite unbearable. And it is that very word that drives people to believe that living their life *is* unbearable and so turn to, what they also believe to be, the only solution. How sad that they couldn't have waited just a little longer, perhaps until someone could show them that there is another way, to tell them that the true meaning of *unbearable* is a state perceived by our own thoughts, not of our being. If we ask ourselves what it is that's unbearable, the answer is, of course, pain.

Physical pain is just a very small part of our human suffering but because it involves the nervous pathways on a physical level, it's very difficult for us to control. Certain people do of course control their perception of pain to enable them to either block it or reduce its ferocity. Such people as those who walk on hot coals and lie on a bed of nails do so by controlling their own minds, not by using a magic potion on their feet or back. More recently, the use of hypnotherapy which controls the mind by reaching the subconscious beyond it is being used in clinical practice to relieve and block pain, even as an alternative to anaesthesia. We cannot fail to acknowledge the magnificent potential of the mind, but at the same time we must recognize the frequent encumbrance of its negative thoughts that lie deep in the roots of our suffering.

It is through my own suffering that has led me to understand, not only its true nature, but the lessons and spiritual growth that it offers. But that hasn't come easily. Although for me it was the disability from long-term illness that became the initial focus of my suffering, I learnt to my surprise that I'd been suffering all my life. I have always had a sense of direction and have usually been attentive to my own intuition but somewhere along the way I missed out on some vital details. It was rather like my husband's DIY skills when asked to put together some flat-packed furniture. He was never willing to read the instructions before he started and therefore considerably complicated what should have been a straightforward task. Did he learn on the way? – well, sadly no!

I believe we all come to earth with an intention or purpose to fulfil and, whilst yours and mine may be quite different, we will all return *home* having fulfilled it or not. I am reminded of the teacher who sends the students off on a kind of orienteering exercise having provided them with some navigational skills, a map and compass to find their way home. Those who fail to read the map or compass correctly get into quite a panic becoming increasingly disorientated and lost, as any subsequent clues are now meaningless. We navigate life using orienteering type skills, but those skills are only learnt as a result of living life. We too panic when we lose our way, but not because we have failed to read the map or lost the compass, but because we have separated ourselves from our true guide on this seemingly difficult terrain. The more we panic, the further and further away from home we become, but all we need to do to recover our bearings is to remain in a state of stillness and await guidance, in whatever way it comes.

From early childhood I was aware that I had a purpose in life, but what I didn't understand until later was the extent to which

I would be personally tested – in order to fulfil that purpose. Most children (and many adults) believe they are the only ones who have difficulties in their lives. To add to them is the 'Why me' syndrome which, if allowed to follow into adulthood, becomes one of our most self-destructive thoughts.

I don't recall having felt sorry for myself during my childhood any more than when I was a fully mature adult, but I constantly questioned – why so frequently I found myself – *out of the game*. I can only liken my feelings to those of a gifted footballer who has been penalized for his conduct during a match and had to sit out, whilst his teammates play on without him. I don't even know anything about football let alone enjoy it, but on the occasions I have seen this scenario I seem to have a built-in empathy for the feelings of the poor chap. For the footballer who finds himself out of the game, the reasons are usually well understood since he has broken the rules during play. The consequences of his actions were also understood when he took them, but his choice to risk both his own career and let his team down was his choice to make.

I was clearly making choices too, as we all do in life, but so often our choices are uninformed and virtually made in the dark. My tears were rarely tears of self-pity because I was quick to realize that didn't bring about change or solution. My tears were those of frustration and anger, believing that I (as the talented footballer) was not allowed to utilize my skills and fulfil my full potential. I knew what I had to give and how to give it, but was being physically stopped from doing so – *I was out of the game.*

I've never been a quitter and neither had I allowed myself to be still and do nothing. There is a tendency in life to envy those people who can just keep going regardless. They don't seem to need sleep and invariably exude an energy that (although exhausting to watch) is capable of carrying others along with them at the same time. They are usually highly focused on what they are doing and they are constantly driven by their need for perfection. Interestingly, the perfection they seek is *never* attained – not because the goal is not achieved or unachievable but because their need lies constantly beyond the original goalpost.

As I write these words, they come as if describing the characters in a book I have read. I feel slightly removed as if back in my dream state, only to be unkindly awoken as I remember the reality of the main character as she now opens her eyes and views life from a very different perspective. When I first heard those words 'Let Go' – they were powerful and yet gentle and compassionate but, most of all, they became the key to my search thence after. How simplistic these words sound and yet, as I began to explore their true meaning, I realized they meant rather more than – pack up and run.

What was I letting go of – hopefully my pain and suffering because I'd surely had enough of that? It then became clear that I couldn't just let go of my suffering, but I could stop it from occurring in the first place if I could let go of what was causing it. This was the time when I began to understand that what I had believed to be the obvious cause of my suffering was, actually, so far from the truth. To be without physical pain, to have my energy restored and to feel well again would surely eradicate my ongoing pain? But I needed to remember that I hadn't become *dis-abled* overnight. It had been creeping up on me over years and because I had resisted the message so many times before… I now found myself in a place with nowhere else to hide and nowhere to run.

Chapter Thirty-One

So – we don't need to have physical pain or sickness to suffer. In the past this word had so many connotations for me, seemingly representing the elderly, poor, sick, disabled and disadvantaged folk. The thought of ever believing it to be something I may personally experience was never one for consideration.

Most of the Western world suffers needlessly on a daily basis due to the way we live our lives. Actually, we don't live life – we suffer it. We suffer because we resist – resist life – resist *what is*. We are constantly either trying to change *what is* or frantically trying to stop *what is* from changing. I certainly don't have all the answers but, like many of us, I had never questioned the way I was living my life in terms of what was happening in it until I was forced to because all that I believed to be *me* had fallen away, leaving me exposed and vulnerable. There truly was nowhere to go any more; no work or projects to lose myself in; nobody dependent on the help I was once able to give; no more complicated strategies to help me climb out of this hole I was in. All that was left was me in my raw state – no frills – no masks, just totally *me*. There was no more to do than to sit and wait. Sit and just *be* – as the resentment, the anger, the sadness and, most of all, the fighting – began to lose their hold.

This process didn't happen overnight or during a magical moment with my mentor or master. It took the entirety of my life until I was awoken – through the intensity of my unrelenting pain. I wish I could say how easy or straightforward it was. I wish I could say that from that day forth I have never looked back, but both these statements would be false. The journey has been tough and the lessons hard, but yes, the way *is* simple. Actually, it is the simplicity of my *new way* to live that has made it so difficult for me. You see, I never did 'do simple' – what was the fun in that? What sense of achievement comes through knowing how easy it all was; how do we pat ourselves on the back for that? But even knowing where I was going wrong and seeing how self-destructive the way I was living was, old habits die hard and as I have discovered – when faced with a 'crisis', we meet it and deal with it using strategies that we are most familiar and comfortable with, regardless of their effectiveness. Familiarity gives us security at a time when everything is falling apart. We cling to it like a child clings to its dummy, forever putting off the day when we can be without our old support systems. It's a brave one who is prepared to go back to the beginning and re-examine their path and the choices made on it. It's a rich one who can stay the course.

If we really want to change our lives and experience joy rather than unnecessary and repeated suffering, we do have to start at the beginning to discover just when things went wrong for us. Let us first look at the wondrous occasion of the birth of a baby. The event of procreation in the entire animal kingdom is such a recurring miracle in life that *gifts life*, let alone the beauty of the birth itself. Whenever I am in a sombre mood and perhaps lacking faith, I only have to remind myself of this daily miracle to be restored. That tiny perfect form that seems almost magically to make an instant connection with most of us is so much like any other baby animal and yet, still to develop *thought*. All external stimuli are perceived by the five senses – sight, hearing, touch, taste and smell. Like any other animal, the baby also comes with a sixth sense – a sense that cannot be demon-strated physically but one that connects the outside world with the *inner being*. It is this sense that has been shown to alert an animal to danger or even connect to human thought and intention. It is a sense that has been put under scrutiny by scien-tists, psychic investigators and psychologists alike, but the truth is that it is just there – an inherent part of us that most of us will have been aware of at least sometime in our lives. Perhaps one of the most significant difficulties for researchers is that, unlike other physical senses, the sixth sense does not originate in the nervous pathways but the spiritual one. The five senses provide us with information about the physical world whilst the sixth keeps us in touch with its own source – our own essence.

But the baby who becomes a child, now exposed to an increasing number and variety of external stimuli and experiences, enters a new world. As he develops language skills with which to communicate in his new world, so do his thought processes develop too. Never again will things be quite the same. Almost overnight it seems our baby has woken up in a very different place. His self-identity has changed from *being* to *thinking* who he is. Within a very few years, our young child has embarked on an outward journey, ironically – to discover who he is on the inside. Within the confines of his physical body, this little being now experiences himself on the continuum of the great wheel of life. With no going back, the momentum of any wheel is experienced in accordance to the effort applied and the resistance exerted – a smooth journey or a hard toll. It is the hard toll that most of us choose at least, until we are fortunate enough to realize we do have a choice. We spend our lives almost waiting for the next hump on the road, as if by so doing, we can put our foot down and stop the wheel from turning. This is why I say, 'we don't live our lives but resist life' – more often than not with our eyes closed. Why is life so difficult for many of us?

Rarely does a day go past when the media provokes just that thought in us. Why do some people have such a rough time of it and why are some parts of the world hit more than others? We may believe we have many answers. Much of the world is plagued by war, drought, famine and disease and our doctors, scientists and theologians alike offer their wisdom in the hopes of delivering so many from what must seem a living hell. Whilst we can do little to prevent some of the natural disasters from happening, we can find ways of preventing the misery caused by their aftermath. We can find solutions to prevent famine and disease, but until we address the cause of suffering in ourselves, how can we know the suffering of others? Until we address the cause of suffering in ourselves, how can we identify and address the causes of our growing family dysfunction, youth violence, religious and cultural intolerance? How can we ever begin to understand the world around us before we know ourselves?

Chapter Thirty-Two

However many books are written about our spirituality, we have to come to terms with the fact that nobody has all the answers. Discovering our own spiritual truth is a lonely road and yet one that is largely dependent on others we meet on the way, so what do we really mean by *spiritual truth*? I have pondered on this question so many times and yet, although I find it difficult to express verbally, I am at peace with an inner knowing that is forgiving of my lack of intellectual expression. It seems wrong to raise a question that I can't answer, and yet, from that admission alone perhaps emerges a clue. We speak of my truth or your truth because the wisdom we unveil at any part of our journey can only be embraced by the traveller on that road. But the journey to discover our own truth doesn't stop there. We have new terrain to cross and with it new experiences which, whilst enhancing the previous ones, may throw us into confusion once again when the light falls on a different part of our track. There is nothing purer than truth so our eyes must be very gradually acquainted – lest they are blinded by the brilliance of its illumination. Our life's purpose cannot be mistaken for our spiritual truth; it is our life's purpose – to remember that truth. It is for us to live the truth of our own journey; to take that of another may be a step backwards of our own path.

Any young person leaving full-time education with a clear concept of what he or she wants to do with their life is often regarded with envious respect. Wherever we live in the world, we have to plan our lives to a certain extent otherwise we will miss the opportunities that life offers us. If those who live in a country where fish is the main source of nourishment, clearly, the fishermen amongst them must plan to fish at the optimum time or their families will go hungry. They must mend their nets before the next trip or the fish will slip through them. But in the Western world, our hours, days, months and years are spent planning. We plan for what we believe to be our purpose, and when we have either achieved or abandoned that which we were planning for, there is nothing left, so we start looking for another *purpose* to work towards. There is nothing wrong with planning for an achievable objective. Indeed, we encourage our young people to plan their lives, but what happens when the plan doesn't go to order? We never prepare ourselves for that scenario because it is regarded as being negative at the onset and clearly (as has already been mentioned) if we set out to do something, we must have the intention to succeed. But how many of us are able to anticipate the excitement of the ride, regardless of the outcome, trusting that we will have profited greatly for our efforts? Life rarely rewards our efforts in the perfect way we want it to, but our inner guide that led us there extracts with precision the lessons of enrichment for our soul. Life is a 'spiritual journey' but only too often we give, what has almost become a cliché now, our casual lip service rather than our dedication to its truth. It has taken me sixty years of searching, questioning and suffering to discover that life isn't a crisis, a competition or even more poignant – a race. I'm not even going anywhere. If I desire (as frequently I do), I can just sit in life in perfect harmony with that of which I am a part.

Truth is truth. It is the absolute state of what is and we come into this world never knowing anything else – until we are taught untruths. I still recall a memory of my childhood when I was so rudely enlightened to the real truth about Father Christmas. To discover from a school friend that my father had been lying to me for so long was more than I could take. I wanted to put my hands over my ears and pretend that I hadn't heard the truth confirmed, but it wasn't merely the non-existence of Santa that was so upsetting. My own acceptance of truth had now moved goalposts. Everybody believes their father, don't they? So now we have truth being questioned by trust.

Over the years I have chosen to accept the mystical figure of Father Christmas as, indeed, the true spiritual expression of Christmas itself – being its truest meaning. On our spiritual journey we frequently make our advances through experiences that seem the least *spiritual* in nature. A child will rarely associate Santa with any more than the wonderful old man who magically knows what presents will delight him or her, but the true spiritual energy that is aroused within each child is rarely identified as more than *seasonal* exuberance. The joy of a spiritual celebration of any religion or culture can be shared, not only by its members, but all those who open their hearts to the joy of others. We stand apart only in our minds, but the joy we feel for each other is the expression of our spiritual connection and the beautiful energy therein. That wonderful energy has no culture, race, religion or politics. This is the same energy that is aroused between people during hard times, crisis times, wars and disasters. This is the universal energy – *Love*.

My acceptance or rejection of Santa's real truth was just one of the many choices I've had to make, but I don't think I've ever been so aware of these choices or of those available to me until I started to review the road I had been travelling. So rarely are any of us perfectly satisfied that every step in our life has been for the best. A frequent admission in conversation about one's own life is that: 'I should have gone to college; studied law; continued with my music'. Many people have regrets about all sorts of choices they have made, particularly when they find themselves apparently unable to fulfil that missed opportunity any more. I suppose I've been very fortunate that there has been no part of my life that I wished had been different – until life started to stand still for me. To have wished to change anything that is past is really a softer way of admitting regret. Regret suggests a much greater sense of self-understanding and thus learning, whilst to have wished it different somehow doesn't own up to our own responsibilities. It would be untrue to say that I haven't had many heartaches on the way and many, many times wished that I didn't have to be put through so much suffering, but there has always been an inner knowing and gratitude for the growth opportunities – be it after the event. It sounds as though I greeted each new challenge with the expectant delight of another new learning opportunity but, of course, it was quite the opposite. I know now that if I had trusted my intuition more, life would have been a lot easier on me and, to some degree, would have spared me some of the aftermath. Interestingly, trust is not the word I should have used here because I've always known of its guidance, but when I didn't like what it was advising – I preferred to try it my way.

No one can tell us how to live our lives or what choices to make along the way, so why do we look to others when we find ourselves in a difficult place? Perhaps the answer to this is that we sometimes believe that someone else *can* show us the way – just as we often believe that we can point out the right path for others? Perhaps we can help by offering advice based on our own experience; assistance from a trusted friend or advisor may be instrumental in the success of our search, but the wisdom that is so generously given doesn't teach us the way – it facilitates our path. The more knowledge we gain in our lives the more discerning we may become with our choices, but we must remember that the wisdom of our soul can only be accessed through the window of experience. The learned professor is not necessarily a wise one, but one with much knowledge. We can read many books and seek all the masters, but we will never find what we are looking for without first finding our self. Then shall we transform knowledge into *wisdom*.

However sorry or even remorseful we are for poor choices, we cannot change anything that went before. The future is only a projection of now and unless we change now – we will continue to regret it in its passing. And everything does pass. As the day turns to night and the river flows under the bridge – all within the birth and ebb of the ever-moving wheel of life itself and with it – passes all suffering and all pain. But so must we remember that one day, one moment, the last of our opportunities passes too and we can never be sure quite when that time is due to arrive – in the present moment of *Now*. Now is the time to surrender to our own being; now is the time to dissolve our own suffering – not tomorrow. Yesterday's tomorrow is yet upon us and never will arrive, for the only moment we can live, learn, love and forgive is this very moment of Now.

PART TWO

Chapter One

My oncoming sixtieth birthday wasn't anticipated with quite the same feelings apparently experienced by many of my friends of the same era. Their feelings of fear and pessimism as though life was now on a downhill spiral are perhaps indicative of the way we perceive ourselves in life. The reason we are sometimes perceived by others as carrying the burden of our advancing years isn't due to ageing lines or greying hair but our own endorsement of that which our minds have convinced us. The many centenarians amongst us now still exude the vibrant energy of the life that they embrace. Sometimes our bodies fail us and we may not be as agile or physically capable as people even the same age as us, but every minute of every day in our lives is as valuable as the one before. The length of time we spend in a physical body is never by chance but design. It's up to us to embrace the gifts that it offers. It doesn't matter how long we live, whether a few days, years or many – life is for living – for experiencing – for remembering.

I had always known, so confidently, that the year itself would hold an element of change for both my daughter and me, but I didn't know why. Strangely, as the year approached I began to get a clearer sense of my intuition when I felt so urgently that – this would mark the year of great transformation. The feeling was somewhat similar to the time when I knew it was right to become pregnant – now or never. Part of what I was sensing was not particularly pleasant. I had repeated images of life just sliding away from me whilst I had another image of renewal and healing. I had no idea what was awaiting me or indeed what opportunities may be on offer, but I knew there would be a choice to make that would affect the rest of my life, one way or another. I had long understood and experienced that healing occurs on different levels. The many cancer patients that allowed me to share their journey had substantiated this when, despite their inability to overcome the sad fate of the disease, I was witness to many of their deepest healings. We mistakenly believe that healing means cure, but it is so much more meaningful than merely the end of a disease or illness. True healing penetrates the core of suffering to ease the pain at a much deeper level than what appears at first to be the obvious cause.

I'm not really sure what happened. I had diligently practised my daily meditation which increasingly gave me the clarity of mind that I was seeking, and inspired me to take the steps I did. My health was already showing signs of change, although a long way from what might be considered recovery. The doctors clearly felt they could offer me no more than moral support and I decided that further consultations with them were becoming counterproductive for us all. As I sat for hours in the various consulting rooms, I began to perceive these visits as not just a waste of time but a waste of my very precious life. I think my decision was received by the doctors with a sense of relief, as their own thoughts and my projected feelings of the inadequacy of medicine could not be disguised. For me, it was just a commemorative ending to my sixty years of life and, on the other hand, a celebratory and exciting start to the first day of the rest of my life.

Inspiration usually comes in a flash and if we take too long to consider it before taking action, it can disappear as quickly as a dream. The realization that no one was going to give me a magic cure was something that I had long known, but I refused to give up hope until I stopped any source of contact with those I had previously believed would finally deliver the magic pill. This was a daunting thing to have done and even on my way home from my final appointment, I wondered if I had been too hasty or even foolish. One always has that niggling fear that as soon as you've walked away, a cure would be found and you won't be there to hear about it. It's a bit like people who religiously do the lottery every week and the very time they forget to buy their ticket, the routine numbers they have always used come up as a winner! But it wasn't just the medical profession I was separating myself from. The support groups, that after much resistance I had finally joined, were sadly to have their subscriptions withdrawn. I say sadly because I believe such organizations play a valuable role in helping sufferers with a common condition by sharing information, giving each other support and relieving the desperate feelings of isolation. The cancer 'drop-in centre' that I worked in was a prime example of the much-needed support given to people with life-threatening diseases. Without that support, many would have been denied the opportunity to exchange experiences and express their own emotions within a safe and positive environment – at a time of their greatest vulner-ability. The support organizations I was now leaving had been my lifeline too, but it was time for me personally to question their benefits versus their disadvantages. The word 'support' is one of varying meanings, but the experience of *being supported* for any length of time readily becomes a need that perhaps removes rather than nurtures the personal drive to explore the boundaries and overcome the difficulties on what is, always, a personal journey. When we begin to identify ourselves with any burden that we carry we are much less likely to discover a way to shed its load. For me, the sense of freedom and joy, having made myself accountable for this daring decision to be truly on my own, was liberating, but my inspiration didn't stop there.

Over the years I have learnt to meditate, mainly by diligent practice and the help of the occasional teacher. The greatest part of my learning though has been through the constant questioning of the many experiences. It was whilst coming out of an unusually profound meditation when I started to consider the experience I had just had and to question exactly what was happening during that process. I was feeling so free and separate from my body that I had no notion of its pain and fatigue and, although I was so tranquil and serene, I felt energized at the same time. Why couldn't I be in this state forever, and what was it that I should seek to harness to help me block out my suffering? Any belief in those last few words would indeed prevent me from any real progress. Surprisingly, I didn't really believe that was what I should be aiming for, but many of us are misguided by the belief that that's all we have to achieve to stop the pain. It's a reasonable conclusion to come to since to be relieved of raging toothache we first reach towards the medicine cabinet. Oh such relief when we can get back to sleep or continue whatever else we were doing, only to forget the very temporary nature of the remedy that blocks out the pain. The *root* of the pain is still in residence just waiting to repeatedly attack its unsuspecting victim, until we are finally driven to seek a permanent solution.

Meditation isn't a daily 'fix' meant for 'bliss junkies' and 'chill outs', yet those who practise regularly begin to regard it as an essential part of their day. I can honestly say that when for some reason I am unable to take time out to meditate, the day seems different, disjointed or even fragmented. My regular practice becomes as spontaneous as cleaning my teeth or brushing my hair and it's not too easy to forget to do either of these things. People who I have assisted to meditate over the years tell me, how much more in harmony with life they feel when practising regularly. I am not a meditation guru and therefore not qualified to interpret the experiences of others or, indeed, guide them to more sophisticated planes. The quality of our spiritual advancement is dependent upon its own freedom to express itself through our own physical channel, the licence of which can only be surrendered through our lone journey of truthful self-enquiry.

And I was hopefully on my way to a discovery when, like a dog searching for its buried bone, I tried to establish the difference between meditation and hypnosis. I had actually made quite a few self-discoveries on the way, least of all to realize that the meditation practice I had been doing for several years was in fact a 'prop' to help me escape the pain, rather than an instrument to help me face it in order to understand it. There's nothing wrong with using a prop to get us through a difficult patch as long as we recognize it as such and don't become dependent on it, beyond its useful purpose. When we break a leg we need crutches to help us regain our mobility, but unless we throw away the crutches when the bones are healed, the muscles will never work efficiently again and the leg will always be dependent on support in some way – never functioning as its true purpose and to its fullest potential.

Increasingly I have realized how many people are under the same illusion that I was, believing what they practise every day – to be meditation. I have introduced people to the foundations of meditation practice many times, when they learn the prerequisite of relaxation and this is as far as many want to go. They think they are there – lovely colours, varying pictures and a deep sense of relaxation often accompanied by soft dreamy music or the verbal guidance into a dreamlike state. I have thankfully long since appreciated the true benefits of meditation, which is of course just the opposite to escapism. Sitting patiently for hours trying to maintain a true state of awareness, rather than semi-consciousness, has not only been difficult for me to achieve, but even more so were the lessons learnt through its achievement. There is a curious nature about life, the relationship we have with it and the lessons we learn from it. I wonder how many of us are constantly unaware of what other jewels of wisdom lie within those lessons, when we believe we've already reached the grade. We could perhaps be forgiven for making such an assumption. After all, how do we know how delicious an orange is before we have tasted one? But having once tasted, let us not be misguided by the belief that all oranges taste so sweet.

Our spiritual path seems to reveal itself to us at exactly the right moment. The only responsibility we have in that process is to be open at all times to receive it. If we shut down, refusing to believe there could be more, we fail our life purpose and 'return home' empty-handed. However, once on the road to discovery, in our eagerness to uncover the next gem prematurely we may mistakenly try to force the door which isn't yet ajar. As with the roses that blossom within perfect timing of their season, so do we have a perfect season that will reveal our true beauty – our absolute truth.

The deep sense of relaxation and dreamlike state that I enjoyed for so long was utterly rewarding in every way. I was able to accomplish a state that permitted me to, temporarily at least, leave my body and free myself whilst indulging in a somewhat euphoric state before, sadly, waking up to the harsh reality of my pain filled, exhausted body. The party was over yet again.

It was after one such blissful moment that filled me with a need to discover how I could harness the state I experienced and bring it into my physical domain on a daily basis. There was another part of me that believed I could actually bring about a complete reversal of all my suffering, and I became more and more intrigued with how my energy fields were really working. I knew that I could truly discover the real qualities and meaning of 'letting go', but I seemed unable to maintain that state for long enough to allow my body to heal, in the way I knew was possible. My mind was flooded with thoughts – thoughts of other ways of achieving that state by assisted means, but in the quickest possible time. Drugs and alcohol were, I suppose, possible fleeting solutions, however, I was not looking to disguise the pain any more but to rid myself of it completely and permanently.

I didn't know the reason for the urgency at that time, but I became almost obsessed with the value of hypnosis. I have no more idea now than I did then where this idea was coming from. The many demonstrations of staged hypnosis that I'd seen on the television I found both uninteresting and demeaning of its participants. But here I was, becoming as preoccupied with finding out how hypnosis worked as I was with understanding the barriers of the human mind, but in this case – my mind. Something told me that I needed to kick-start my body to start functioning normally again. I believed that it had lost its way and needed to be reminded how to operate efficiently once more. I believed then as I do now that my body had 'got out of sync', as they say, and somehow needed to be fine-tuned. The more I thought about what my own body needed to restore it to order again, I also began to think about something that I'd never truly understood about the healing I gave to others. People have asked me so many times to explain some of the strange phenomena they would experience during healing such as the heat or tingling they felt through my hands, or the waves of energy pulsing through their body. On one (more unusual) occasion, a woman experienced these waves so strongly that it made her physically sick. I could never explain the process to them, any more than they were clearly identifying themselves. They were feeling the energy channelled through me to them. But sometimes, I am guided to start the healing with some gentle but seemingly powerful words that I now believe prepares the mind to prepare the body to accept and utilize the healing energy being channelled.

So now I had to research – not a hypnotist but a hypnotherapist. At least I would know I wasn't going to be given a glass of vinegar, believing it to be wine or worse! After a long search my efforts were finally rewarded. I was faced with a directory of hundreds of therapists whose credentials I had no way of checking, except from the impressive bios they had written about themselves. Once again, my limited knowledge about the subject had implanted (perhaps justifiably) a fear about the possible detrimental effects of hypnosis. Just about to close my laptop and admit defeat, a name literally jumped off the page at me as if highlighted above all the others. Within half an hour I had made an appointment with a man whom I still knew nothing about, apart from what I read on his website, and yet I felt strangely at ease with my choice. Bill, a practising Buddhist, was a clinical hypnotherapist already working in health institutions. What really got my attention was the personal story behind his career when he had found himself in a life-threatening situation. In agonizing pain with a broken leg, he waded in the river whilst dodging the gunfire of the war zone he'd been working in. He was left with few options to secure his safety, and pain being his major burden – there was only one way to deal with it. He survived his ordeal by stepping beyond his thinking mind and thus the intensity of his pain. It seemed that Bill had applied self-hypnosis to overcome his pain, but hearing about the way in which he dealt with it had triggered all my own memories of the way I too learnt to lessen my own intolerable pain. I had no idea that I may have been using self-hypnosis, but the way I was identifying with his story made me even more determined to discover if he could help me, and besides – his practice turned out to be less than twenty minutes from my home!

As I approached the house I became rather hesitant and nervous, wondering if this was really a good idea or if I should turn around and go home. How strange the way unfamiliarity plays tricks with our minds, making us feel vulnerable and uncertain. I lived so very near to the area that I was visiting but in some respects it was as though I had just crossed over an invisible divide represented perhaps by a difference in wealth, but most noticeably one of culture where there was a predominance of Asian population. Even the shops were characteristically Asian with beautiful sari silks in one and perhaps another stacked with wonderful spices. As I walked up the street trying to locate the house I was visiting, I felt distinctly vulnerable and yet strangely excited at the same time. I had lived overseas in some intimidating environments and had always been at ease making friends, despite the obvious cultural differences. What then was my feeling of unease now, just because I was seeing a predominance of men and women clad in their own cultural dress? At the time, I was so intrigued by my own heightened senses that I was yet to question why people sharing the same culture are attracted to the same environment, rather than explore a new one. How was I perceived in another country, living in the tight-knit community of my own people? These were observations that I felt quite uncomfortable with but had alerted me yet again to the real hurdles of our spiritual journey called *fear* – a topic that I will come back to later.

As I found the house amongst the terrace of other rather uncared for looking properties, I climbed the steep path to the door at the back. As the door was opened and I was greeted with the traditional Buddhist bow, a serene and calming aura reached out to me in an almost ethereal way. My previous anxieties had dissolved in seconds, rather than minutes, and I began to absorb the peace that was radiated not only from the man in front of me, but seemingly from the very fabric of the four sparse walls around me.

As we entered the therapy room, the absence of a comfortable couch was rather disappointing. Having noticed a suitably comfy-looking therapy chair, however, I felt that I would at least be able to relax at will if the state of hypnosis didn't happen. It was then that I realized I was surrounded by exceedingly high-tech equipment that just didn't fit in with my idea of hypnotherapy, let alone of the serene Buddhist. At first glance, I felt that I was in a recording studio rather than a therapy room. My mind was so clued into what I had envisaged this place *should* look like and how it actually was, that I was near to admitting a mistake. My mind was in judgment mode, having already decided that I had wasted my money and, much more importantly, wasted the precious energy that I'd hoped to restore rather than diminish. My thoughts were so angry, negative and judgmental that only a tranquilizer could surely quieten me enough to let the process commence.

So what happened? I remember observing with some interest the words that had almost seduced me into the stillness of my own being. I remember knowing that I had been to this place many times in my meditations. I still recall with clarity the similarity of the hypnotic words chosen by Bill and those that frequently left my lips whilst I was giving healing to others. I was seeing, feeling, experiencing and yet my body was so relaxed that I was totally unaware of its presence. The session was without any forceful suggestion in terms of my own self-healing and yet the renewed feelings of optimism and hope were overwhelming. The intense physical pain that I had expected to interfere with the therapy had seemingly dissolved, at least for the time being.

I was puzzled when after just the second visit Bill suggested that I didn't need any more sessions with him. I still had symptoms of pain, extreme fatigue and muscle weakness that I had come to unload and yet, strangely, I was not disappointed and fully accepted his judgment. I didn't go away with a heavy heart because, on the contrary, something within was moving – I could actually feel it. I'd had this feeling before, after receiving healing; not a spontaneous cure but a feeling that I can only describe as a profound shift at the core of my being. There was indeed an intense shift within me now. This was an energy shift or, more accurately, an energy exchange, and I was sensitive to its very nature. That was why I didn't need any further help from Bill – the magic had already taken place and I was now responsible again for keeping it maintained.

My experience with Bill had not been that of the stereotype hypnotic trance that I was probably expecting. I hadn't been led down the path of reflection to discover where my illness had come from in the first place, perhaps delving into childhood traumas and so forth. And yet, I *had* entered a state of trance that was totally familiar to me and whilst I was in that state, I recall being asked to see healing light permeate my body. I remember thinking how unnecessary that was since some sort of presumably healing energy was already coursing through my entire vessel. In the softest of tones, I recall Bill's voice reminding me of the choices I had between anxiety and calm, between illness and health. How many times had these words been delivered through my own lips? Reluctantly, and somewhat resentfully, I was brought back more swiftly than I'd preferred to the reality of my own physical body.

Chapter Two

Within a few weeks I was feeling so much better that I was already beginning to forget how ill I had been. The process seemed to improve as the days passed, something that surpassed all my expectations. My friends and family looked at me in disbelief. The feeling was perhaps akin to the initial introduction of cortisone that I'd been taking for fifteen years before having it slowly but cruelly withdrawn, when its side effects were actually causing the symptoms that it had once treated. Withdrawal of cortisone after such a long time is a potentially dangerous process, not to mention the devastating withdrawal symptoms. I was told that my adrenals would never function properly again but I knew that they could. Finally coming off the drug that had been my lifeline was a miracle that I knew could happen; my determination and faith in that belief eventually paid off. But *now*, my renewed status of health and energy was almost too good to believe.

It wasn't long before I was battling with another brain-teaser. How could I forget, so quickly, quite how bad things had been for me for so long? It wasn't that I didn't appreciate my new freedom but a few weeks suddenly felt like a year ago. I felt like a wild animal released after captivity, subsequently having almost forgotten its way home and excitedly darting this way and that, trying to pick up the scent again. At one point, I wondered if I would need some more therapy to help me understand my own confused emotions, but the feeling of urgency connected to all the events soon made itself understood.

My house was up for sale. It was far from an easy decision for either me or Katy since we had lived in the same house in Marlow for twenty-three years – almost all Katy's life. We had many wonderful memories which felt now as though they were part of the fabric of the place, and even knowing that they would all come with us, we both struggled to separate ourselves from a previous life. We knew that it was time to move on, but far more important than the change of scenery was the fairly urgent need to find a property that was more 'user friendly' for someone whose body was rapidly failing her. Although I was perhaps more ready to leave 'Hillcrest' than Katy, I privately wanted to relieve her of the caring role and let her be free to develop her own career without the concern of my needs. When the house went on the market we didn't know of course of the forthcoming changes, but curiously enough, despite our failure to sell the property or to be inspired by anywhere else to live – we kept to our plan. The estate agents were as amazed as us that the house didn't go within the first couple of weeks. There had been plenty of house viewers keen to spend an hour or two over a cup of tea (or stronger), but not so keen to part with their money. I've never really understood the mentality of professional viewers, but like everyone else in the mode of selling, we couldn't be too critical of their interest – be it a hobby or for real. Strangely, neither of us felt too pressurized and on more than one occasion considered it a signal that we were perhaps not ready to leave.

Looking back, I don't know why it seemed to take so long to find a suitable buyer when, actually, it was only a few months. They always say that a house is sold when the time is right and never were these words more apt than for us. It was as though someone was just waiting to place the last piece of the jigsaw as soon as the other relevant pieces were in place. The dramatic improvement in my health seemed to change everything. I felt that I could do anything I wanted to and that was a longing that had been well and truly suppressed until now. Katy had returned from the supermarket, ready for us to enjoy one of our frequent impromptu chats over a cup of coffee and a Danish pastry. But that wasn't the only unremarkable practice of the day. She had yet again found it necessary to relate her experience of people's lack of courtesy and inconsideration to each other, which she found almost intolerable. I sat quietly in my usual sympathetic mode whilst trying to demonstrate the futility of her wasted energy, but this time, her true feelings were expressed in words that I wasn't expecting –

"Let's go to France, Mum."

So many family memories had taken place on our numerous trips to France. Richard would have loved to have moved there if Katy hadn't been so settled in her school. She and I had often spoken about the possibilities but after Richard's death, commitment to our menagerie would have made it difficult. The deterioration in my health would have made it unthinkable. So what would hold us back now? Well, with four ageing dogs and two cats – was that not a reason to stay on home soil? How could we possibly transport all of them when they were so unused to travelling? It was all so easy to put obstacles in the way and yet that wave of almost excited urgency sent my mind into overdrive. I recalled the large open spaces and idyllic old Périgordian houses. I smelt the baguettes, still warm from the boulangerie. I felt the freedom and a quality of life that I inwardly yearned for – yes, everything would change if I could only be brave enough to do it. Katy, now clearly sensing a weakness in my resolve, continued to deliver the words that quashed every objection I raised. My heart was racing with the sort of fear that was akin to the first (and only) time I jumped off the diving board at the swimming pool. Katy's voice now fading into muffled oblivion, I could almost hear the chant of unseen faces – Jump! – Jump! – Jump! I could bear it no longer – what was holding me back, apart from my fear? All I needed to do was jump, but this wasn't to take a leap from fear but indeed – a leap of faith.

Chapter Three

It was never my intention to include anything in this book beyond my wonderful healing. However, as the deepest part of me flows through the channels of my hands I know the story has yet to unfold its true meaning and, indeed, its obligation to those reading it. But these are not self-help chapters on how to survive in a foreign country, any more than my story of struggling with ill health. This is my reflection on the lessons gifted to me and the self-discovery that takes place in any survival process. These are teachings that could have been delivered in the home I had spent twenty-three years in or on the other side of the world, but something higher than me had to be sure that I would hear; like the child who is sweet-talked into the doctor's surgery, only to find a painful injection awaiting her. No sweet talk was required to encourage me to taste the fruits of foreign travel once again. I had entered with my eyes wide open – or so I thought.

I don't know why Katy and I always spoke about *us* or *we* going to live in France. We both knew that she wasn't coming and the laid-back Dordogne was hardly the place to work on her new denim label, besides it not being her choice of permanent abode. Maybe the anticipation of goodbyes and our complete change of life after such a long time under one roof needed a more gentle approach? It was not long before we unexpectedly found ourselves living on the opposite sides of the globe, so perhaps on some level we were preparing ourselves. Leaving the nest is part of the natural process of growing up and becoming independent. It is something that many mothers, in particular, grow to dread, and a milestone that young adults greet with enthusiasm, until they've tried it. It always felt to me as though there was an element of role reversal for us because it was me who would effectively be gaining independence again, and there were no guarantees that I would make it. Katy, on the other hand, would follow a path that would prove more challenging than anything she had yet experienced – physically, mentally, financially and, more importantly, spiritually. Her story is not for me to tell; except for you to appreciate my own reasons for feeling as though I had abandoned ship – but I knew *this ship* – wouldn't sink.

It seems almost impossible to stand back from our loved ones' problems and challenges in life, but for me that was perhaps even more difficult than for many. The Buddhist teachings on attachment, or rather detachment, are not difficult for me to achieve in relation to material possessions, but to stand back from those I love has been one of my greatest challenges in life. I believe now that this was the real reason for me taking the leap and coming to France. Standing back from loved ones' lives is just another lesson in letting go, but that doesn't just happen automatically with enforced separation from *whatever* we are trying to detach ourselves from.

The first few months in France could easily have proven to be a big mistake. However, there were no disappointments as yet with my new lifestyle, but for the obvious grief that I shared with my daughter as things for her seemed to go from bad to worse. On a practical level there was little I could do as the days became weeks, whilst she waited to take residence in the little flat that we were buying for the purpose. I was now committed to our six animals and being a new arrival made it difficult to find a pet sitter. 'France is just across the water', I used to say to my emotional friends before I made the transition, but now as I waited daily to discover where my daughter had spent the night before... it began to seem a million miles away. The mobile bills were mounting up as I seemed to be constantly topping up in fear of losing my only contact with either Katy or, indeed, the solicitor in charge of the flat conveyance. Meanwhile, she was trying desperately to keep the start of her new business venture afloat. What made us take that leap – faith or maybe – just stupidity? These were the questions I had no doubt were in both our minds now, but there truly was no going back – at least – not yet.

They were not happy days and life was filled with uncertainty, yet my health was still amazing. I had energy and strength and the restrictions of temporary accommodation in the small gite I was renting before finding a place of my own was strangely liberating. With just the animals and me in one room, the dark evenings and cold days of winter descending upon us was quite surreal. Without television or Internet, I felt as though I had walked into a dream that I would no doubt awaken from. But I didn't and as the days went on and the months ticked past, so did reality finally check in. I was really here in France, but in my own house now – for which I had total responsibility once again. What an adventure!

The flippancy with which I have used this word is somewhat inappropriate since my real understanding of adventure has only recently been revealed to me. I have always needed stability (perhaps leaning towards permanence) in my life; my Taurean birth sign being questionably accountable. It's quite surprising that I have these traits since I've enjoyed travelling and change so much, but it's always been necessary for me to be able to make a nest, wherever I am. This nesting desire has at times proved to be an expensive one. Wherever I went, my precious books had to accompany me, whatever else I left behind. I remember relocating to the North of England for a year whilst doing my teacher's training. I had a tiny room for lodgings but still insisted on loading my little car to the roof with books and then wondered why the suspension had gone! It's so easy to blame our own obsessions and inadequacies on the stars we were born under, the parents we were born to or even the circumstances we were brought up in. We don't have to take responsibility then and if we fail to recognize where responsibility lies, things will never change and we will continue to blame circumstance for anything in life we don't achieve or don't like. Our attitudes are, of course, not only formed but also changed through the many experiences we have in life. But can our attitudes and perceptions be considered faults? How about my desire for permanence and stability – is that a 'fault' or a weakness? Maybe it's not only others whom we judge too readily but more importantly ourselves, because our judgment of others is directly influenced by the way we perceive ourselves. When we are uncomfortable with ourselves in any way, we automatically judge others accordingly and judgment is something that folk – particularly in the Western world – do so well.

Chapter Four

Whilst *adventure* seems to suggest a journey of new and exciting experiences, it also has a ring of impermanence to it. When I was in the Middle East, I knew that I wouldn't be staying there permanently so I was able to experience my stay as a wonderful adventure; whilst at the same time, allowing myself enough permanency to build my 'nest' – for as long as it was required. The excitement of children anticipating a holiday is so delightful, but listening to them recall their many stories upon return confirms the nature of their wonderful experience – an adventure for sure. But isn't that what life offers us all, every minute of every day that we live?

I didn't think of my new life in France as an adventure, exciting though it was. I could only see it as a new life that would offer total freedom within its beautiful terrain, and the challenge in becoming part of that new life was thrilling. I didn't give failure or returning to my homeland a second thought. I was effectively emigrating – for good. How very strange I thought it was that people should come to live in this beautiful place and then want to return home. I was even more fascinated by the people who really didn't know how long they would remain French residents and were happy to enjoy permanence, on a daily basis. I don't know why but this discovery made me feel distinctly uneasy when I first arrived, although it was short lived once I had friends who seemed to have established themselves more permanently.

Wherever I have travelled in the world, I have never turned my back on Britain, always thankful for its many virtues. But I hadn't come to France to escape Britain, I had come to find myself a better quality of life, or so I thought. Was I sure I wasn't trying to escape and if so, from what? Why would I think my quality of life was going to change when I was already relatively privileged, living in a lovely house with a spacious garden in a Buckinghamshire village? What did I really expect would change and what really had I come for? In recent months I have addressed these questions with great diligence, searching my soul for the truth therein. How fortunate and how blessed am I to have the opportunity and the freedom to do just that and *that* – was the answer to my question.

I am reminded of the emotions that welled up in me when making the decision to take the great leap of faith and move to another country. I didn't make it lightly. I just knew that it was a choice that I would not regret. When Katy and I listed all the positives and negatives of coming or staying, the quality of life was high on the agenda, but it went beyond just changing a materialistic environment for one of natural simplicity. I needed distance and thinking time, quiet and stillness, reflection and peace. I wanted to leave all my anxieties behind me and I was sure that an environment that could afford me absolute isolation, should I desire it, would be mentally and spiritually nourishing. Even as I became the victim of the second to highest cause of stress (house selling), I visualized my absolute freedom away from everything and everybody that might interfere with my search into my very own soul. As I sat on the bare floor of my house, now deplete of all belongings (still awaiting the phone call to say we had sold and could head to the port) – I was pacified with the anticipation of my reward of tranquillity. There was a *knowing* and an urgency deep within me that counteracted all thoughts of fear and failure, but the freedom I was seeking, I was yet to discover – was something I would have to earn.

Chapter Five

Familiarity breeds contempt, so they say. I'm not sure that is always right but certainly, once we are familiar with our surroundings, we can become more content. Coming to a new country is no different than entering any new situation, although of course, I hear you say – on a slightly different scale maybe? I have always had itchy feet after a certain period of time in any particular situation, despite my Taurean traits, but that didn't mean I necessarily wanted to go globetrotting. When Richard was alive, we had a few near misses resulting from both our desire to keep the estate agents in business and having the entire country to choose from, now that he was retired. The grass it seemed might just be greener in Cornwall, Dorset, or even Cumbria – but was it? I can't answer that because thankfully we woke up just in time, when an uninformed buyer for our house decided that 'exchange of contracts' was his cue to renegotiate. It was our cue to question exactly what it was we were looking for by moving from a place we already had made our home. For the first time only in twenty-three years, I had asked it of my dwelling place again.

For many people, the thought of remaining in the same house for that length of time would be quite unbearable and I have friends who, in better economic climes, would move every five years or even less. To me, that would have been unbearable – at that time anyway. Familiarity brings an added sense of security and wherever I go and whatever adventures I have, I will always return to a familiar and welcoming base. I think we all need a base in life. Why then did I accept the challenge of moving home, not just within my homeland but to another country, another culture, and another language? Surely it would have been easier to continue to stay safe and enjoy the adventures of my foreign holidays?

To say that I had itchy feet was to put it mildly. The sense of excitement that was generated from the anticipation of a new start was almost uncontainable. However, every enticement that I had perceived as a good reason for moving to France, I now know – was not my soul purpose but the carrot offered in order to get me to accept a much deeper challenge. The challenge wasn't to learn the language or survive the summer heat. It wasn't to live in a culture that I would struggle to perceive accurately, owing to my deficient language skills and different values. My challenge was to do no more than *be* in a place of stillness and fulfil my own purpose – the purpose of my soul. And my soul knew the perfect location in which to remind me, direct me and show me that which I knew, but had temporarily forgotten – nevertheless – my purpose. As I write these words, I am reminded of the clarity with which they arrive, through the stillness of my being and hush – of my own ego.

Chapter Six

I spent a whole year free of all pain and generating enough energy to run a steam engine. Surprising myself at the ease I could scale the stairs and even thresh the long grass in the overgrown garden, I had forgotten quite what is was like only the previous year. What I hadn't forgotten, and was forever thankful for, was the miracle that had enabled me to travel to France, let alone live there. Having previously been unable to travel even the thirty miles from my house in Marlow to London, I am left to ponder the true nature of my healing. For some reason, after that magical year my body abruptly reminded me of its previous weaknesses, sending alarm bells ringing all around me. For a few weeks I revisited the place I'd once endured for so long, as I questioned once again the nature of this change. Probably sooner than it seemed, I began to improve, although never quite recovering my former energetic and totally pain-free self, until now anyway.

I have spent many hours meditating and even praying in the hopes that I would find answers about the cause of my relapse, but as yet the mystery still keeps its silence. What wasn't quite so silent was the response to my emotions of sadness, frustration and hurt, when I suddenly realized how very fortunate I've been. My pleas for answers turned to prayers of thanks; thanks that I'd been made well for long enough to accept the challenge and come to France because that's the way I perceived it. My temporary state of almost self-pity had turned into rejoicing and thanks for every blessing I could possibly think of, but this wasn't a conscious decision. The words just flowed through my lips without warning, for what may have been as long as an hour. I am still in pain and my muscles weak. I am still unable to physically fulfil all that I would like, but I am still giving thanks and rejoice every day for all my many blessings. I no longer spend my precious hours seeking answers and looking for more but I am ready to receive them, if and when they come. My body still hurts and yet I know healing has reached every part of me and will continue to do so, if I remain receptive to its guidance.

When deciding to make another country your permanent home, everyday living is challenging enough. I remember in Kuwait when I had to meticulously plan the week's menu beforehand because there was never a guarantee that we could buy certain food – somewhat nerve-racking at times. Trying to get a suitable menu together for our high-ranking Japanese visitors would have been daunting enough on home ground; not knowing if even a tin of sardines was available was just too much for me! When the supermarket shelves accommodated the European palate, it wasn't for long! Certain products disappeared for weeks on end before being flown in again, so everyone stock-piled, aggravating the situation still further. I remember during my pregnancy developing the most unfortunate craving for smoked salmon. I could have chosen all kinds of foods that were readily available but I needed salmon – at eleven o'clock at night! My poor husband – I can see him now. Having first scanned the supermarket freezers he then checked the hotels, to see if they would sell him a plate of smoked salmon for his pregnant wife.

Even in France I find many things that were freely available to me in England are not to be found here. In a part of the world where the word *vegetarian* is treated with disdain by most meat-eating Frenchmen, my culinary imagination is appropriately exercised and frankly – exhausted! Having a fair experience of the country before coming I wasn't too surprised by some of the differences, but I still find it interesting to look back on my first days here. The observation that most intrigues me is how quickly I began to feel at home. If you ask anyone what is meant by *'feeling at home'* they will probably speak of feeling comfortable, content, safe and, last but not least, feeling welcome.

Everything that makes us feel that we are in familiar surroundings, even though we have just moved ourselves to unfamiliar territory, suggests home. I had no doubt at the time that France would remain my home – perhaps influenced by my need for stability and permanence, thus supporting the saying: 'Home is where you make it.' The real truth, I have finally learnt, is not 'home is where you make it' but 'home is where you are'.

When I first arrived in France, for at least the first year, everything was very new. Finding out where to buy the most mundane things; how to carry out everyday operations such as paying bills; sending post or even how to write a cheque was all part of feeling familiar with my surroundings. Interestingly, half the time I just stumbled across many of the things on my *how to do* list rather than anticipated them, as most organized ex-pats seemed to. The feeling of oblivion was wonderfully peaceful but my awakening to that oblivion was a rude one. My understanding of what we politely call 'bureaucracy' paled into insignificance when working with the real live model! Why couldn't I just switch payment of my electricity bill from one method to another? Why did I have to wait months on end for the tax office to pass my residency declaration to England, thus forcing me to pay tax in both countries in the meantime? Why did I have to give three months' notice to change my insurance company? Was anything straightforward in France, I began to wonder? Strangely, that is how I began to perceive every new encounter – as a hurdle to be cleared.

I am familiar now with the peculiarities of the everyday running of things, and I have an opportunity to stand back and observe where I've come from. Long gone is the serene mood that came with my naivety; indeed, the awakening to the real world could perhaps be equated with that of the child we looked at earlier. I moved from a period of feeling at home to a feeling of displacement and uncertainty as I failed to be able to anticipate what had once seemed straightforward. I have learnt that there is no general pattern of expectation and response in France and when you think you've 'got it' – another unexpected turn is thrown in. I have now reached the contented state of familiarity, but with the acceptance of few expectations of certainty any more. I love this country dearly and although still unable to communicate on a level of deep conversation with its natives, I truly do feel at home again – so why would I want to leave?

Chapter Seven

I have very real and practical reasons for going back to England. The one that surpasses all others is the ease with which I will be able to see my daughter on her trips back from America. There are several other reasons that would lure me away from this wonderful environment and every one has been carefully considered and weighed up against the benefits of staying. I am now as certain as I was when I ventured to come – that the time draws near for me to leave, but not before taking with me everything I came for.

I sit here now in the tranquillity of my surroundings, feeling the gentle mood of autumn as it announces its approach with the dewy mornings, cool evenings and slowly changing colours of the trees. This morning I was even aware of the lovely smell of the burning timber that was glowing in a nearby neighbour's grate. How I would yearn for that experience in my own grate. Long before I ever thought about coming to France, walking back through the village of Bassenthwaite after a long day's hike on the Cumbrian fells my senses filled me as they were fed with the welcoming smell of warming fires. Enjoying now the comfort of my own log fire, I am so filled with all the things I will miss – knowing that so much of it I cannot take with me and, yet, the inner calling to return to England is too strong to resist. Over and over again I remind myself not only what I will miss of France, but how different England will be after six years or more away. The space, the tranquillity and the freedom to just *be*, with almost as few commitments and obligations as I choose, is not something I envisage recapturing in England. I have long been intrigued by the desire of ex-pats (from all over the world) to return to their homeland and now, it seems, I am intrigued by my own longing once again. I am quick to check my reasons in case the reward is a figment of my imagination that I may live to regret. I have to remind myself that whilst not impossible, it is improbable that once I have gone, coming back is unlikely. I needn't feel that I have failed the test any more either for I know now – I never was meant to stay for the duration of my life. I came to complete a journey – in which lies a story.

Chapter Eight

Part of the excitement of coming to France was my dream to offer a Spiritual Retreat for people to come and escape their busy lives, receive healing and have an opportunity to get in touch with themselves in a beautiful and tranquil setting. I had no idea of the difficulties that I would encounter to enable me to do this, hence my intentions being diverted through an easier door. Life constantly presents us with obstacles to overcome on our spiritual path, but it is in the overcoming that is relative to our growth and advancement. Life, however, also closes doors on us and to try and force them open results in no more than pain and regression, rather than joy and growth. We need to understand the significance of a closed door and rather than banging at it any harder, seek for the one that is already a little ajar – almost in expectation of our arrival. In truth, this clearly was not the primary reason for coming, but one that I now realize disguised a more personal need to *escape* – in response to a much deeper calling. My near envy as I heard of those around me going on personal retreats to the Himalayas and distant sacred places was a calling to find myself too. I have long understood that such a haven isn't necessary to satisfy the source of that longing, but the complete commitment to identify the source is. I have also long realized that in our endeavours to escape, we run further and further into that which we had hoped to be freed from, and further and further away from the truth we are seeking.

When I first came to France, life was so difficult for so many reasons that I found myself constantly praying to be given the strength to ride the waves, and meditating on the qualities of that strength. I had, it seemed, escaped nothing. I had merely brought all that I was running from to a different environment. When I worked as ship's nurse on board a passenger liner, I observed with great interest the relationship difficulties between couples and families as they approached their final destination. The excitement and anticipation of a new life as they sailed the seas to Australia became their imaginary new life itself – until they neared the reality of their dreams. The country they were heading for wasn't a panacea for the broken or fragile relationships they thought they had left in England – and so the panic began to set in, before they even disembarked. Fulfilment of our dreams isn't a spiritual or any other kind of gift. The gift is the opportunities we are given to enable us to find a way to that fulfilment, from whence emerges the joy of our self-knowledge and spiritual advancement. People emigrating to Australia or any other part of the world may well be blessed with the gateway to opportunities to live a dream, but the dream itself will not become a reality until they use all the tools they are given to make it so. I had been gifted with a window of perfect health to come to France, but it was mine to discover the real purpose of the gift.

As time went on, and some of the bigger issues started to settle or were overcome, I found myself more content with my surroundings and my place in the new life I was living. Even with the loss of three of our beloved dogs (who seemed to make a habit of taking their leave to 'higher places'), the rewards of my environment were beginning to live up to expectations, as the peace within me became more receptive to its own gift.

In life we have so many opportunities, regardless of our wealth, culture, or religion. The opportunities will of course be different for all of us, even within the same social strata or family. However, opportunities are worthless when they go unnoticed or unrecognized for their true value. Many of us live our lives failing to see all the open doors around us. We are so busy imagining the *perfect* life which we see ourselves moulding that we miss the mountain of gems that has always lain beneath our feet – just waiting to be invested. How regretful we are when someone wiser and more attentive than us toils to clean them up and reveal their real beauty and value. We miss those treasures every day of our lives, and some of us spend an entire lifetime never knowing they were there for the taking. I so nearly missed out too, but this time – on the greatest opportunity that would lead me to the place I had been seeking all my life. I so easily nearly returned to England with the thoughts that I had made a mistake, but for a few nice memories to take with me. But I needed more than memories, and although I had now reviewed my experience as a long holiday rather than one of permanence, something was still not right.

I have always known intuitively when something isn't right; it's the energy I sense around me and within me, but frustratingly, I rarely *see* the complete picture. I've had this experience enough times to know that it's not a good idea to just plough on regardless.

Desperate for calm and clarity once again I sat in meditative mood, gazing into the forest, the birds chirping around me and the squirrels leaping in joyful play from one tree to the next. I sat like this for several hours without intention, just letting my mind still as my vision fell on the beauty of nature all around. I became engulfed by that same beauty; feeling its presence in the *oneness* of my own existence in *all* that surrounded me. There was no mental effort, just a feeling of tranquillity and peace that preceded a sudden burst of joy. A moment hit me like a flash of light, when out of the stillness of my own being emerged what I knew to be – *my truth*. My entire time in France to date was a final opportunity to *see* everything that had gone before, and whilst I had spent time envying the spiritual experiences of those in a mountain cave somewhere, I suddenly understood. That was exactly where I had been and that... was what I had come for. I was on a *spiritual retreat* – the truth of which had made its self known through the urgency of my writing. I was returning with no lesser an awakening than if I'd have been in physical isolation in a mountain cave. But it was in my own isolation yet again that had revealed it to me, in the stillness of my *being*. I had come full circle and this was – *my epiphany.*

Chapter Nine

Some people are utterly scared of isolation or being alone for too long. Observation of others on their spiritual pursuits over the years has taught me just how many of us are affected by that possibility. Although I love people and company, I find it hard to have my space invaded for too long. I have already mentioned my post on a world cruiser as the paediatric nurse; the opportunity to fulfil such a sought after post being a fascinating story itself. At the time, I was waiting to fill a post that would enable me to devote more time to my parents. Having surrendered my resignation for the post I was in, I was shocked to discover that my new employers had changed their minds! For the first time in my life, I had to consider myself as unemployed and as if that wasn't disturbing enough, I still couldn't discover what the reason for their rejection was. Did I need to experience the real meaning and feelings of degradation that occur as a result of unemployment I wondered? How my heart goes out to those who find themselves in this place.

For me, although it seemed much longer, it was thankfully a short-lived experience. At the time, in despondent mood as I scrutinized the nursing press for suitable posts, my eyes were drawn to a vacancy as ship's nurse. I don't know why but I knew this was for me, even though experience had shown me otherwise. I persisted for two days trying desperately to register my interest but the scarcity and appealing nature of the post resulted in blocked phone lines. Disappointed but ready to face up to reality, I made one more last attempt to call; the rest of the story has already been revealed. There were in excess of four thousand applicants, but the post had always had my name on it – as in my soul, I somehow knew. The nurse carrying out my vaccinations before I sailed recognized my name as the person who had been due to join her team as district nurse. She was also good enough to tell me that a well-meaning GP, knowing my motives for wanting the post, had acted not against me but for me, when he rejected my application. I have wondered many times if this man could have any idea of the catalytic effect he has had on the rest of my life, just through that simple action?

The glamour of sailing the high seas was far overrated, but the many difficulties and adjustments of life on board were far exceeded by my need for personal space. How more isolated could I feel amongst the hardened sea travellers and the alien environment in which I was now living? I shared a cabin with an Italian girl who spoke little English. We were in each other's presence for much of my precious time, when I wasn't working the long hours in the hospital. Uncomfortable though these conditions were, I was greatly rewarded with the delights of visiting places I could only dream about before. Finding a place for quiet contemplation, however, was like seeking a blade of grass in the desert.

So what is it that makes some so desperate for constant human company? When we fear being alone with ourselves and our thoughts, we seek to ease that fear by filling our lives with other distractions and commitments like the workaholic. Isn't it the same as those of us who start planning the next vacation even before returning from the one we are enjoying at the time, when summer is over it's eyes down for Christmas? Do we ever give ourselves a chance to enjoy what we have right now? The answer to that is no; we can never be in this moment whilst we look constantly to the next. But why do we do it?

We don't usually live our lives consciously but, if we did, we would see how little we are engaging with it and therefore getting out of it. It is only when it's pointed out to us, often through what seems at the time a misfortune, that we are stopped in our tracks – frequently by force. When we are taken from our own environment and put into one that is alien to us, we are alone with ourselves. When we seek the solitude of a mountain cave, it is to be – *alone with ourselves*. We can be alone with ourselves by choice or by circumstance but neither is a quick path to our spiritual truth, unless we are prepared to *meet our self* on the journey. When we truly meet our self for the first time it can be every bit as frightening as we first envisaged. After all, isn't that why we have not dared to venture down this route before – when fear repeatedly keeps us from opening the door?

This is probably the first time in my life that I have truly met myself, but now that I've been brave enough to take the challenge, it almost scares me that I may have passed through life in complete oblivion of my own identity. "All the world's a stage," said William Shakespeare – and we are all the actors in it. How true this is for most of us until we finally separate ourselves from our physical existence to progress into the next, by which time – it's too late and opportunity became but a passing ship that took no passengers. I have often felt as though I were looking in upon that stage, like a silent witness to the unfolding plot, just awaiting my cue. But now I stand within me – witness to my own being – my own essence.

I love going to the theatre to watch a play. I love to feel the energy of the people around me, all there to experience the words of the writer's script as they come alive, according to the skills and interpretation of its actors. I love that energy so much that for a while, as I join the audience departing through the theatre doors for home, I manage to keep it with me, brief though it may be, before getting into my car and entering my *other world* once more. How wonderful it is to escape into a world of fantasy; then I'm alerted to the ambience of the theatre and take a while to ponder

– not only on the fantasy of the play I saw, but the reality of the energy I experienced. The energy of our essence en masse allowed expression, whilst we focused on the stage – through the space between our thoughts.

What is it that stops us looking further? What is it that we don't want to see? How many times a day do we glance in the mirror to check our appearance or maybe somewhat vainly admire ourselves? Sometimes we are merely making sure that we are presentable, and all too often, we don't particularly like what we see. We even forget ourselves that the added lines and grey hair is a poor indication of the person we are. How many of us look into that mirror and look beyond the image that is reflected before us? Maybe we feel too uncomfortable to linger any longer, but in truth, we will never hear the answers that so many of us seek until we befriend our own reflection more sympathetically. When we glance into that mirror we have no intention of seeing further than the outer shell. We may examine the wrinkles or check the smile, but when we look more searchingly, more deeply, we will see something quite different. When we earnestly discard make-believe in the quest for truth, we will see ourselves as if for the first time – as never before. I thought I knew all about being in touch with myself. It is, after all, a phrase that is so commonly used by those on the road of spiritual enquiry, but I wonder now how many others have shared the belief that they have arrived at this all-important point? I know now that I had made good progress, but actually, had only just arrived at the gate – having resisted the invitation to walk on through. How do we know when there are more steps to take if we have no idea what's at the end of the path? From the moment we start formal education we are given a structure to our learning and guide-lines to assess our progress. We have a teacher to show us the way and check that we understand the lesson. When we are travelling anywhere we use maps to guide us, and as long as we don't deviate from the map, we can expect to arrive at our destination. But our spiritual path is quite different. We may see signposts on the way but the only measure of our achievement comes from within. There are no gold stars for trying or certificates of attainment to proudly display. My father's favourite saying to me was:

"In life, you never stop learning."

These were probably words of great wisdom but our spiritual journey is not so much to learn as to – help us remember.

I have worked for many years as a spiritual counsellor and facilitator, helping others to explore their own spiritual path. I choose the word *facilitator* rather than teacher because whilst we hope that a good teacher will facilitate the process of learning, we also expect him or her to provide the lesson for learning to happen. Our spiritual journey is one that lasts a lifetime and beyond. We should remind ourselves once again that the only lessons we receive are those that help us *remember* and not a course of excellence to be passed. We are not under any obligation to satisfy targets to qualify for bonuses and we can choose to take as long as we wish, before progressing to the next stage. If we want to take time out without reprisal or get off the train at the next station and just admire the view, we can, but *the journey never ends*. I can only share with you what I know today; tomorrow I may view it differently, the higher up the mountain I climb.

If our spiritual path is just one of remembering, why do we seem to find it such a struggle to do just that? Some of us have difficulties in remembering all sorts of things, least of all where we have put the car keys, important papers etc. My mother always relates (what became an amusing story after the event) how she left me in my pram outside the fish shop and didn't remember until she arrived home without me! I was always puzzled how a mother could possibly forget her own child and was hesitant to accept her excuse that: "You were such a contented baby, I just forgot you were there." The truth is of course that my poor mother had so many other things to think about that, being so good, I clearly wasn't one of them.

When we forget a past event or perhaps forget where we put the car keys, we run through some sort of checking process in the hopes of jogging our memory, but we do know what we are looking for, making recovery more likely. Even more interesting is the importance of the lost item in relation to our determination to find it. Clearly, we can't drive to work without the car keys, or get a divorce if we've lost the papers. Why is it that we can't seem to attach the same importance and commitment to finding ourselves?

Some of us don't place any value on our real purpose in life. Even when we believe we have identified what we are here for, as we have already seen, it frequently becomes no more than a goal that we want to achieve rather than an ongoing journey we want to explore. We often strive for more money, acquisitions, promotion and leisure time. We seek for perfect relationships, readily discarding anything that doesn't fulfil our idea of perfection, whilst forgetting the true purpose of those relation-ships. We seem to be striving constantly for something other than what we have or who we are. Even children from the earliest age will proudly announce their intention to *become* a farmer, teacher, builder, ballet dancer or singer. The list is endless, but the desire is still the same: 'I want to be something other than who I am'. We seem to be almost driven to reach for something that is not yet within our grasp and by which society judges us accordingly. But how mistaken and how ill-informed are our judgments, as we fail to realize – who really is in the driving seat.

We are indebted to the many men and women who, seemingly driven by their own inspiration, have contributed to great planetary advancements at all levels, but inspiration isn't a driving force. Inspiration is the guiding force of our own spiritual essence that works in gentle harmony with our thinking mind, but like intuition – first fleetingly appearing in the moment between thought, but *never* in it. For as long as we maintain this sense of balance – inspiration, intuition and clear vision flow effortlessly, but when we fail to honour that harmony we fail also to keep open the channel through which it flows. It is our soul intention to experience itself within the restrictions of the physical body, utilizing the beautiful instrument of our mind to discover itself, as it plays with its physical environment. We are designed to test our natural potential by expanding our boundaries and fulfilling our purpose – for the greater good of *all* mankind. But mankind is failing his own test when he ignores the voice of his true essence and enters a delusional state believing – *he is his physical body*. When we believe that of our own identity, so too shall we believe it of all human beings and thus become embroiled in the common fantasy of illusion without even knowing it.

Chapter Ten

For as many years that I have tried to assist others on their spiritual journey have I searched into the depths of my own *being*. So continuously have I questioned – why I was not more at peace myself when I could help others to discover theirs? How could I help facilitate the process for others without being able to apply the wisdom I gave them to my own journey? It is only with the passage of time that I have understood the deficit in my own understanding. When I am working with others, my absolute focus and compassion for that person allows me to become the perfect channel to receive and deliver the incoming wisdom or healing, without even thinking about it. Unfortunately, my willingness and dedication doesn't give me the automatic passage of right to solving my own problems. I have to work much harder at that. It's only after many years of observation, questioning and determination that I'm on my way to keeping my channel free, allowing that wisdom to flow readily for my own advancement, but with those lessons comes a new under-standing. It was only ever my mind that stood in the way and, sadly, still does at times.

There is a saying that goes – 'The teacher is only one step ahead of the student', and my teaching days often substantiated that belief. I think one of the reasons why I've always enjoyed teaching so much is the special relationship between the seeker and the teacher, but even when working with children, I soon discovered that this was not a one-way process. Indeed, I have learnt as much from those whom I have taught (in whatever domain) as I have given, and my life is greatly enriched by those relationships. We are all at different stages on our spiritual path; and as thankful to receive the assistance of the one who ascends before us on the mountain as we are humbled to offer our hand to the one who follows so closely behind. Along the way are many pointers. All it takes so often is that little chink of light to illuminate a very dark passage, but if our eyes are closed – we cannot see the lamp. We have to be receptive to the limitless divine energy and power available to us, but in order to use it to its full potential, sometimes it means – *retuning*.

'What came first – the chicken or the egg?' This is a profound question that seems to be almost unsolvable and, yet, so many of the problems and issues we face in life seem equally unsolvable. It isn't until we perhaps rephrase a question or come to it from a completely different viewpoint that the penny drops and the answer comes to us. When teaching a child who just isn't 'getting it', a good teacher will try to assist his understanding by presenting the lesson in a different way or using different words. What a wonderful feeling it is for both pupil and teacher when the child suddenly *sees the light*. Some of us seem to be naturally adept in taking a different viewpoint when we want to solve or understand something, and those of us who can do this are blessed with a great gift but it's an attribute that can be learnt, providing we become open to all possibilities. When we're faced with something we don't understand we have an automatic tendency to see it one way, but the more we focus our minds on that way, we will never see it any differently. We are effectively stuck.

'When is a chair not a chair?' – *When we see it as a tree*. I remember some years ago just relaxing with a cup of coffee whilst sitting in the armchair before my coffee table. I don't recall thinking about anything in particular, which admittedly was unusual for my overly employed mind at that time. Suddenly and without any warning, I saw the coffee table completely change its form. At first I became quite scared because I thought I was overtired and my mind had tipped, but almost as quickly I realized that I was experiencing the true nature of the table – which was not even a tree but raw energy. Nothing quite like that has happened to me since but as fleeting as the experience was, it taught me a precious lesson to aid my road to enquiry. Although it was unintentional, I had temporarily retuned my mind to the higher vibrations of my own essence, without which – I cannot experience beyond the reality I touch, hear, smell and see – a reality of a dream state. Beyond those attuned to our physical senses are many realities but for us to lift the veil that hides them, we must first discover the nature of the veil.

Chapter Eleven

The nature of our *being* gives us the potential to become perfect receivers of our very source and yet so often we choose, knowingly or not, to block the flow through our channel. It took me many years of quiet patience to understand my father's profound fear of anything vaguely mystical. Such was the belief system that had been enforced upon him in childhood; this intelligent, thinking man stayed for most of his life in complete denial of his own identity. Denial of our spiritual nature is like denial of the cancer we may suffer, there really isn't any difference. There is always such a waste of both energy and opportunity when we deny a truth that we *know* is there because, at some time, we will have to face and accept what is constant and can't be changed.

Denial of any truth never comes from our spiritual source but from the part of us that is constantly trying to gain power over us. We have seen how early the young child puts aside the purity and oneness of his own existence, believing himself to be quite separate from life around him; already he thinks he can mould and dictate to life itself as he tries to make it his slave, rather than his friend. 'My life' – isn't that what we say? Just recently, during the time when I believed I had really cracked it, something happened to me that I thought had effectively destroyed *my life*. Everything I had overcome, discovered, learnt and healed, all that I now looked forward to was finished – abandoned. Someone was unexpectedly about to become totally dependent upon me and become a large part of my life. And they were.

At the time my brother was diagnosed with terminal cancer, we had been estranged for two years. Learning the news, I was shocked – probably numbed actually. I don't remember giving a second thought about helping him except perhaps to wonder how he would receive me after our estrangement. Love is truly unconditional. Forgiving and reaching out to him at his great time of need was a wonderful healing for both of us. My brother's sad and dramatic plight touched me at my very core and, as it seemed to me at the time, there was no question as to who would care for him. My brother also lived in France, having been a lone resident for many years. There would be many challenges for me, faced with not only the cultural differences of care and protocol, but also the limitations of my language skills, let alone the sibling differences I may still have to face. Jeff's eyesight failing rapidly whilst his brain was losing its function, the frustrations, the heartaches and the tears were yet another story, as I tried to make sense of both his and my own suffering. How can we ever truly share this journey or any other, with even those closest to us? I never knew what he was really thinking or indeed if he had moved beyond the prison of his thoughts – long before his departure. Our life experiences and our suffering alike can only be perceived in the solitude of our own presence, but it was the kindness, support and generosity of my dear friend Jeanette Clulow and my doctor Roger Nguyen that took the loneliness from my journey. There were many folk supporting me, not least my own family and friends in England and of course my daughter. France and England once again seemed a long distance apart. But it isn't my purpose to relate the journey I shared with my brother over the next eight months, but to return to one of the greatest lessons revealed by that journey when I spoke of – *my life*.

At the time, the reality of my commitment to Jeff was emotionally and physically challenging and I'm afraid to say, temporarily left me feeling somewhat resentful and sad. It wasn't that I didn't want to care for him and share with him the last months of a most precious journey. It was my own misunderstanding of what and how that changed life for me, but the greatest gift was when I realized I had it all wrong. I didn't then, and never did, own life – none of us do. Nothing had actually changed except the sad physical status of my brother and even he was not leaving *his* life. I was momentarily frustrated that all my life plans were forcibly on hold. I could well miss out altogether as my body, already stretched to its limits, may fail to survive its new challenges as I became exhausted both mentally and physically. Repeatedly I reminded myself that no one had enforced this upon me. I had a choice and without any second thoughts, or indeed regrets, I had taken the action that I wished to take. So why the resentment – why the confusion?

When things don't go to plan for us we all have moments of emotional turmoil. We often revert to our childhood status of metaphorically 'throwing our toys out the pram' in a sort of feeble attempt to enforce a change of circumstance and appeal for help – any help. In truth, we are helpless to change anything and really we know that, but we never seem to address it and learn from it. We can't plan our lives because we don't have a life to plan. We don't own a little empire that is apart from everybody and everything around us. We are but a tiny ant that is part of something much, much greater, but only – part of. We cannot dictate a pattern to life. We can't manipulate or cheat life, but we can envisage a path that we ourselves *intend* to fulfil and create, within the life we live. Frequently, the nature of our existence and that of life around us will change the route we take, sometimes considerably. When we become aware, we know ourselves as a part of life rather than the rulers of all life. We will greet life and all that it offers us with joy rather than disappointment or sadness; we will begin to go with the tide rather than try to row against it all the time. When we stop dictating and battling, we begin to know and to trust that all experiences gained in our physical existence are yet another attribute to our spiritual whole – which is what we came for.

Several people have suggested to me that 'being there' for my brother may be part of the reason I am in France. We all seem to want to discover reasons why things happen or what purpose certain experiences fulfil. I believe that both Jeff and I have been given a rare opportunity to forgive and clearly, I am as humbled to have had the opportunity to help him as he was, to receive it. Apart from the deep sadness of his journey, I also shared with him joy and laughter. We shared words with each other that we wouldn't otherwise have spoken. Do I think he was part of my purpose of being in France? – No. The challenges of caring for my brother in another culture have given me a new perspective of life, but far more significant is the new perspective of myself that has occurred because of it. When we are out driving in the countryside we often find 'stopping places' offering a beautiful viewpoint. We may drive just round the next bend and the vista changes dramatically, even though we are witnessing the same hills, fields or rivers. Had we not been out for the drive or chosen not to stop, we would have missed a wonderful opportunity to see the passing countryside from a different perspective. I don't believe we should always try to identify reasons for our life experiences, but rather than fight or question – watch and trust, whilst taking advantage of all that it offers. Looking for reasons why something has occurred in our life is our ego once again taking over, but it certainly won't reward us with the answers we are looking for and if we don't ask it to step aside – the beautiful view round the next bend may soon be perceived as ugly.

The non-acceptance of experiences in our lives is a frequent partner of our quest for 'reasons' and is the major cause of our human suffering. We are so conditioned that even the most wonderful occasion is tainted by our mind when it says: '*I don't believe it, it can't be true!*' At the other end of the scale, we have the more unpleasant experiences which are just as readily denied: '*This just can't be happening to me!*' or '*Not again!*' We seem to believe either that life has a vendetta against us and singles us out for bad experiences, or that we are just not worthy of the more pleasant ones. But aren't we forgetting what life is about? Within its beautiful design is the constant changing that *is* life and change – means movement. Even as we sit within the perfection of our creation, it silently pulses with the *life force* that feeds it so that we may experience ourselves, in the stillness of its magnificent beauty. The perfect functioning of every single living organism is dependent upon both internal and external homeostasis or balance, which it is largely responsible for itself. But we don't exist as singular entities. We are all part of the greater whole, interdependent to maintain a balance that is achieved by no more than an orchestral harmony between *all* living organisms, but with only a few notes out of tune having the potential to destroy – an entire symphony.

When we remember our purpose in the orchestra of life our heart sings joyfully, with its every changing note, in true accord with the precision of the conductor's baton.

Chapter Twelve

My brother has left us now for his new life and I am left wondering: what fleeting lesson was it that he came to experience – in the life that had all the potential to offer so much more? Here we have a man whose fond connection with the earth became his daily sustenance. It always seemed to me that the beautiful produce he so lovingly picked to feed himself was nature's reward, in return for the love and respect he gave her. Here was a man who, like many of us, spent his life seeking and searching for its deeper meaning; the search for his own purpose and meaning. How strange it seems that someone with such an affinity to the very soil he tilled whilst responding to the song of the nearby birds as though his children – should still be seeking meaning? How strange that someone who tended passionately the wilting plants in their struggle to survive the scorching sun and drought, who witnessed the thriving lettuces as they competed for nourishment with the stone-filled beds around them – should search for meaning?

As I reflect on my brother's own quest for answers, I feel the presence of his peace... now surrendered to free him of his once troubled mind. But as I recall – I am quietly reminded of his legacy to those he left behind, fortunate enough to have witnessed the meaning of his *oneness* with nature. A oneness that was complete, even though he didn't seem to know it.

And whether we know it or not, we are all searching, searching to fill the gap that repeatedly makes its presence known, between our thoughts and our actions. But we don't like gaps or spaces. It's our human nature to want to complete things and make them whole. Silence is uncomfortable for many of us because it's a form of gap or space. Rather than see what emerges from that space we prefer to turn on the television or play music or even pick up the telephone – anything – to block out the silence and thus the space that could reveal to us so much. When I used to watch Jeff nurturing his tomatoes or tending the pigs, it seemed that he almost blended in with what he was quietly doing. This wasn't something he had studied or learnt to do; this was the transmission of the most powerful energy of *Love*, passing from him to his vegetables or animals… within the *spaces* of his own thoughts. His harmony with nature, which alone came from his empathy with all nature, in turn provided the space for that to happen.

Several years ago, long before I came to France, my brother rang me in a distraught state asking me to send healing to one of his piglets that was just hanging on to life. I'm quite used to this kind of request, but this time I *knew* there was another way. Instead of my invisible hands on the piglet, it would be my brother's direct contact as I gave instructions over the phone. The expression of my brother's emotions as the energy flowed through his hands and the piglet came to life was unforgettably moving. It wasn't the phone line that transmitted the healing energy but the space that carried our *unconditional love*, without which – healing on any level cannot take place. Love truly knows no boundaries, except for the limitation of the space that we ourselves provide for it to flow.

We cannot witness someone else's space, and neither can another person demonstrate it to us. We have to experience it ourselves and, when it appears spontaneously, the beauty of its presence can be awe-inspiring. Most of us have had at least one of those moments that never leave our memory banks and yet so frequently, we want to explain it away or treat it as though it never happened at all. We don't like gaps and even more uncom-fortable to us are the gaps that seem to contain something we can't quite fathom. For those of us who are diligently seeking our spiritual meaning, it is the *spaces* that we need to pay attention to because it is only through these spaces that our own divine energy can be experienced. One awesome experience of *grace* will lead us to believe that the spaces are few and far between, but how far from the truth this is. Once we allow ourselves to be in the stillness that calms all thinking – we will find ourselves embalmed in the *grace* that flows effortlessly through the spaces of our own serene *being*.

As I am inspired to write these words, I am reminded of one such beautiful and spontaneous event in my own life. I was out skiing on my own whilst living in Norway. Considering my limited skills on skis this probably wasn't a good idea but I knew that the family I was living with were at least in the vicinity, should I run into trouble. I *did* run into trouble – quite a lot! I became so engrossed in the beautiful scenery that I lost my way, becoming quite disorientated. But as I stared at the magnificent snow-covered mountains reflecting the rapidly sinking red sun – I became totally absorbed into my surroundings. For however long it may have been (probably minutes rather than hours), it was as though I was almost engulfed by the mountains before me, giving me a feeling of absolute perfection, completeness and yes – *pure Love*. I felt no fear being lost whilst the late afternoon was turning to dusk. I was filled with an overwhelming joy, peace and serenity all at once, whilst the thought entered my mind that, just maybe, this was my experience of what many refer to as – God? Still full of wonderment and almost disbelief, the stillness of the moment was broken by the sound of chattering skiers as they passed nearby, allowing me to follow them to safety. The memories of my encounter with that beautiful state will never leave me, but now, some forty years or more on, I understand its permanence and its accessibility to all of us, as the very essence of *who we are*. When I observed my dear brother growing in his field, I know that I was witnessing a soul who knew who he was – for at least, as long as he *loved* that which also occupied his mind.

Forty years or so ago I was still on the same journey of spiritual enquiry, more often than not, seemingly taking two steps forward and three steps back. There comes a time for most of us when we feel we are making little advancement at all. How I would yearn to share my experiences then with those of like minds, but even as a child I was warned against speaking of such things in case my mental state was treated with suspicion, or more so, how my own father would react. Strangely enough, it was my father with whom I chose to share my moment 'on the mountain'. Writing to him long pages of descriptive prose that never really could express what I was feeling however hard I tried, and yet his response was one of complete compassionate empathy. When we release the love within us, its power is so strong that it is capable of illuminating even the most inaccessible places – no explanations or words are needed – we are as One.

Chapter Thirteen

Since the time when I first consciously took steps to emerge on the path destined for me, I give my humble thanks for all that it has offered me in its direction. Now, as I patiently wait in France for the next phase of the event, I wonder how many of us have trodden this path in solitude, unaware of our silent companions. How life has changed in such a short time. Perhaps with the liberation of women and their rights came, not only an opportunity to be released from the kitchen sink, but a freedom to express the essence of their being and their true purpose. In the nurturing female environment, it wouldn't be long before the male gender would feel safe enough to surrender to their spiritual essence, at least… some of them.

From the lonely path of the spiritual seeker – almost overnight it seems courses and workshops on every aspect of spirituality have emerged, all over the globe. Such a dramatic change would probably support that envisaged by astrologers as a *new consciousness* entering our planet with the incoming Aquarian age. But when something becomes available after a long period of denial and deprivation, we tend to act as if we are receiving food after the famine. We may believe that the supply will dry up, leaving us hungry again, but then we are in danger of becoming 'course collectors', rather than – *collectors of wisdom*. So we have to remember, spiritual growth isn't something that happens to us whilst attending courses and retreats. Our temporary 'high', fed by the equally temporary collective energy of other course participants, quickly ebbs away like the tide unless we acknowledge our own responsibilities in transmuting it into something more permanent. Spiritual evolvement depends not only on what we take from life but what we put into it, and like everything else in life – we have to earn it. Like the farmer's crop in the field, we must feed and nurture it constantly to keep it alive and allow it to grow. Misguidedly, many of us see the easiest way to nurture our growth is by attending another course or going to bed with yet another book – all in the search of the answers we seek. But as with any other course in life, our success is only determined by the homework we do in the meantime.

I, like most, have been very lax about doing my homework over the years. I would go at it with great enthusiasm to begin with and then lose interest – frankly because it was too difficult and took too much time. Just as every problem we face comes with its own measure of difficulty, once we know how to overcome it we forget just how hard it seemed in the first place. I remember my first attempts at learning to drive many years ago. My father patiently (or not so on occasions) assured me that I would soon become 'as one' with this lethal vehicle and not even be aware of what my hands and feet were doing, as they automatically changed gear. I didn't believe him because it was not within my experience at the time but desperate to earn my independence, I thankfully decided to put my faith into his words and continue to do my part to make them transpire. All life's challenges are tests for the soul and without them the soul cannot evolve, which is our only purpose for inhabiting the human body: to experience both its delights *and* its restrictions, challenged further by its own environment. Some, of course, suggest that all souls come to earth for this experience, perhaps as an animal rather than a human being. I'm not ready to consider that one. Maybe, having seen how we treat animals, the thought of coming back as one is too daunting for me. On the other hand, experiencing the deep connection I've always had with them should perhaps make me question if I have already walked this planet in a furry coat or a pair of wings.

I recall one day when a couple who had been introduced to me by a friend rang to ask me if I could help them with their dog. I made all the usual enquiries about veterinary consultations and so forth, before making an appointment to see them. I always see animals in their own environment to spare them the anxiety of being subjected to an unfamiliar one. I soon learnt that this little dog not only had an established medical condition, but also a psychological one. Seemingly, a legacy of the ill treatment he received in his early life before being rescued by his present owners. The dog had become very territorial about them and his new home. For several days before my visit I quietly meditated on the situation in an attempt to connect with the dog. I wasn't sure quite what to expect when I arrived as the apprehensive owners introduced me to their beloved but somewhat unpredictable pet; however, we needn't have worried. The dog, apparently quite uncharacteristically, had greeted me with the enthusiasm of reunited friends. I knew instantly that I had made a connection with him, making it so much easier for me to work. I only visited him once but, to everyone's amazement, following my visit the dog went to a place where his toys had long before been rejected and started to play with them, becoming calmer and less aggressive. I had already warned the owners that my gift was to heal, but not to prolong life. Within a very short time, the little dog passed away peacefully in his sleep.

I don't know what to make of so many seemingly strange and wonderful things that have happened as a result of healing. I don't even know if my presence has had anything to do with these wonders, but I do know that we are as connected to the animal kingdom as we are to the brotherhood of man. If we don't start to acknowledge that and respect them as we would wish for ourselves, we are in great danger. Already, animals in the wild who normally live in harmony with their human neighbours are expressing killer instincts towards humans. I'm very reluctant to assume anything about animals or human behaviour, but when either of us has reason to repeatedly mistrust – the *karma* is written. Animals do have feelings and emotions and yet so often we hear the comment from someone fighting their own cause: 'They wouldn't *even* treat an animal like that!' Need I say more about our regard for the most beautiful creatures of this planet who can, and will in time, teach us so much? Animals are our friends if we allow them to be, but disrespect and abuse of other humans and animals alike only ever happens when we disconnect from our spiritual source. And this is a dangerous place to be, not only for ourselves but for all humans and the entire planet. Animals sense the intention of humans. Kind or cruel, we cannot disguise what we are feeling towards them any more than to another human, because the energy we emit reflects the source from whence it comes – either our mind or our spirit. But within the history of man's own journey to date, we have dimmed our senses, becoming impervious to the energy around us and disconnecting ourselves from our most valuable source of information. An animal's survival is totally dependent on both the energy it emanates and the accuracy with which it translates the energetic field within its environment. We all have moments of heightened sensitivity to the vibrations around us, but few of us are prepared to exploit that gift as the animals do and, indeed, as was always the intention of our design. Once again, our envelopment in the materialistic world disguises us as effectively as the shell of a nut that protects its kernel. The question we need to ask ourselves is: *Who* or *what* is it that we believe ourselves to need protection from? We may be surprised to hear the answer, if indeed we are prepared to tune in – to our dormant receivers.

Chapter Fourteen

As I review the earlier part of my writing, I ponder over the choices I have made and wonder how much pain I caused myself in the process. But we all have choices to make and when the consequences of those we choose bring discomfort to ourselves or others, there is little we can do about it except learn from them and accept, rather than spending the rest of our lives in regret. If we can treat our mistakes as our friends rather than our enemies, we may begin to understand more about ourselves and the choices we make and embrace the lessons within them. Our inability to accept the outcome of our choices retards our growth and causes still more suffering.

I still haven't got my head around the 'New Age' use of the word *karma*. I get quite frustrated every time I hear the repeated phrase referring to someone going through a difficult patch as – *'Oh it's her karma'* or, *'It's my karma!'* Who is it doing the judging here? I often think the word is used as an excuse to accept our own shortcomings, but more significant is our ignorance of its true meaning. When we don't understand things, the human race has a habit of either pretending that we do, or shrugging it off as insignificant. The nature of our karma is clearly determined by cause and effect; what we sow, so shall we reap. Whether we have debts to pay or to receive in this life or in another is irrelevant, but to recognize the immediate consequences of our actions and choices *now* and anticipate the more far-reaching ones is essential to our spiritual growth and – the survival of our species. Although it may seem that way sometimes, karma isn't the 'brownie points' we are awarded for our good deeds or punishment for the bad ones. Karma is the beautiful instrument that guides our soul back to its natural state of perfection, before such a tool itself becomes redundant. The hardest part of man's journey is not how stoically we accept our karmic lessons, but how courageously we seek to discover their real meaning on our spiritual path.

Chapter Fifteen

'If only I knew then, what I know now.' How often have I thought these words? How many of us have thought the same thing, perhaps wondering how we could have done things differently and escaped from some of our suffering? When we are young, life takes on a very different meaning for us and we focus mainly on the short-term goals that we believe are central to all our happiness. Sadly, when we get there we are frequently disappointed as our achievements seem to lose their magnetism, prompting us to look for another goal to head for. Time after time we run towards something new that will make us happy and, because we are young, we call it an adventure or a game. What we didn't know when we were young was the significance of the games we played, as we chased a bright star that seemed to magically disappear every time we got close to it. The sheer thrill of chasing kept us fired up like a kitten chasing a shadow, but like the kitten – we wouldn't notice the terrain we were crossing or how many other good things were on our path, because our only focus was also *illusionary*. And what we didn't know as a child was that unless we were quick to learn, our childish chase for the illusory prize would follow us right into adulthood. A major cause of all accidents is our lack of focus on where we are now, at this moment. The major cause of our discontent and unhappiness is our failure to live in this moment – *Now*. There is nothing on this earth that will *make* us happy. Happiness is our natural state of *being*. We don't have to chase after it; just experience it – in *this* moment – *right* Now.

Many of us are accused of never 'growing up', but this shouldn't be received as a criticism if it refers to being young at heart. Surely, that's where most of us would like to be? But if we are still constantly chasing gratification without experiencing the path on the way, we become spiritually stunted. Jesus said, we should *'be like children'*. In the days when I was trying to find my own spiritual meaning through religion, I never truly understood the meaning of these words and the many other beautiful teachings. But I know now that when we see life with the simplicity and purity of a child's vision, we see for the first time our own essence. When we reflect with real intention of self-discovery, we must become increasingly curious about ourselves and the world around us, indeed, as a child. It brings me so much joy to watch the curious intent of a child as he observes with such open scrutiny a new situation or object. But the child doesn't judge that which he watches, he just watches – often in silence. We too must guard against our curiosity becoming judgmental, either of ourselves or others. Most of us are seldom aware that we are almost in judgment mode all the time; anything, anybody, any behaviour or action that is or isn't to our liking takes on a label – a label of judgment and that judgment says – *'I know the right way to live.'* When we choose to accept things that we either have no power or right to change, rather than having the eternal battle that goes on within our heads, we provide a space for the essence of our own *being* to speak to us and liberate us from all that is *not* us. This is the true meaning of 'letting go', and letting go is the most liberating, non-doing thing we can *do*. Letting go means freedom from the self-imposed incarceration we have endured for so long.

I was giving a talk once about our judgments, when a young woman verbally attacked me saying:

"That would be taking away my right to an opinion."

For a few minutes I needed to gather my thoughts whilst I wondered what to say to her, particularly since she was sparing no judgment of me and was very angry too! Of course there is a close similarity between the two words and we are all entitled to an opinion or to make a judgment, but that doesn't make us right, even though our need to be in control convinces us otherwise. On the other hand, an opinion tends to be made with greater humility and is always soft and usually substantiated by one's own experience. 'In my opinion' we say – which is suggestive in itself that there may be another view – 'but this is mine, at the moment'. When we make judgments about ourselves or others there is an uncomfortable finality about it, which is very sad because it locks all the doors to any other possibilities and therefore any progression. Becoming non-judgmental doesn't mean we condone behaviour and actions that are unacceptable or distasteful to us. The freedom from letting go of our judgments comes from opening our hearts to the numerous possibilities that we have never explored or even thought about before; a freedom that somehow releases us from our egotistical, self-appointed responsibilities. The rewards of restraining our egos and watching as through the eyes of the child, rather than stepping in with our judgmental minds, are wonderful, but never easy to harness without training. Throughout our lives we have to make judgments based on our experiences. A junior doctor wouldn't (or shouldn't) be asked to diagnose or treat a condition for which he has no prior experience because he couldn't make an informed judgment. But we have become almost programmed to make judgments about things, people, situations, and often ourselves – completely based on ill-informed personal prejudices and childhood conditioning, all of which now make up our own unchallenged belief system.

Chapter Sixteen

When I look around me now, I am made aware of the vast changes, not in my life but in my attitude *to* life. I have always been aware of my spiritual essence and yet, strange as it may sound, have frequently forgotten it in my desperate need to find it. It seems that few of us incarnate into a physical body with absolute clarity of who we are, except perhaps some who have chosen or been chosen to carry the light to the rest of us. Did *they* know their true meaning? We tend to forget that even the greatest of our teachers and prophets do not escape the challenges and hardships that life has bequeathed to them. If life was without its difficulties – the birds wouldn't need to sing, the flowers bloom in spring or the dog have his bark, all in the process of living. Life would be still; life would be stagnant – an ambiguity in its self. We need to constantly remind ourselves that the much coveted progress we see in others are the rewards of their diligence and focus to reach out for that reward. We are not all born to become great leaders or teachers, but we are all born with our own purpose to fulfil. To fulfil it from the humble perspective in which most of us dwell is as important as the one who fulfils it in high office. Our misconception of our role in life starts early. As adults, we have a moral responsibility to nurture the child's perception of their own qualities; their own abilities; their own value and self-worth. The many young people in the world who sadly perceive themselves as they believe they are being perceived is a very sad indictment of us all. We must value ourselves so that we shall be valued, but we must first be in touch with our own essence, our own divinity. We all have a responsibility to *all* our children; to fail them is to fail our own purpose and close our hearts, thus denying our true nature and theirs.

Chapter Seventeen

Material possessions have rarely been of great importance to me and yet I can still remember the excitement of shopping trips on a limited budget. Apart from the few occasions when I was accompanied by my mother I always shopped alone, mainly because that's the way I liked it. So that all seems a bit ambiguous too – doesn't appreciate material possessions and yet loved shopping? I don't suppose the 'high' that I would get from my shopping spree was very different from that of the compulsive shopper, but my compulsion had nothing to do with shopping at all. Compulsions to do things are akin to addictions and the reasons we develop these behaviours are of course variable, but always hidden deep inside them is a need – our need, to find fulfilment from something we are unable to truly identify. I became increasingly curious about my own addiction as I sensed the deceptiveness and futility of its nature. I yearned to find stillness inside me, and strangely believed I would find it through my *doing*. It is possible to find the stillness that reaches out to us in our state of *doing* – just as my brother did when engaged in his growing. But it must be a focused state, and that is difficult to achieve if you don't know what to focus on.

Here I am, so many years later, reflecting on my addictive and compulsive behaviour that was finally laid to rest by none other than the product of its own doing – ill health. But it's only now, when I see the truth so very clearly and realize that my constant need to satisfy an even deeper need was not as futile as I had once thought. I wasn't just looking to fill a gap. It was the deepest part of my own essence that was trying to quietly direct me to the place I wanted to be, but I was only listening with one ear, whilst the other remained attentive to the elaborate promises made by my own misinformed ego.

Once we commit ourselves to our spiritual quest, in our enthusiasm we need to guard against losing touch with the very reality
that we hoped to discover. This may seem a strange thing to say
but the tendency to overindulge in all things 'spiritual' misplaces
the reality of our spiritual, physical and mental balance in life. It
should be our goal to discover the beauty of that balance, even
when we are subjected to the harsher challenges of life. It is so easy
to sense the presence of our own spiritual essence when we are
experiencing times of joy, but few of us will stop to acknowledge
our presence within; except, perhaps, when we question its
apparent ever-changing mood. Our spiritual essence doesn't of
course change at all. It is constant and supporting but will always
give us the free will to either experience its constant joy or – the
undulant nature of our mind. It's our unhappiness that accom-
panies the latter, persuading us to search more deeply as we try to
liberate ourselves from the suffering it brings, thus reminding us
of the perpetual wheel we are on. But we do need to accept the
changes and challenges rather than believing that living a *spiritual
life* will solve all our problems and put us in a permanent state of
bliss. We don't have to speak of ourselves as being spiritual, which
is almost like saying we are *being human*. Our essence is our spirit,
our life force, and its purpose is to experience itself on the physical
plane. To decline that opportunity is like the child who desperately
wants to learn to swim. After all the brave excitement he is finally
too fearful to jump in, not realizing that his water wings would
save him from drowning. Unfortunately, so many of us start off
with these misconceptions and it often takes us years of experiencing, questioning and repeated disappointments before
awakening to that truth. Attending meditation classes, lengthy
spiritual retreats or any other kind of spiritual instruction will
never *make* us enlightened, however painful or lengthy the process
may be. The passage to enlightenment is so simple and yet so
difficult for us to attain. All that is asked of us to achieve this
enviable state is to – *open our eyes and wake up.*

Chapter Eighteen

Over the years that I've worked as a healer, I have become increasingly intrigued by the process itself. As I previously mentioned, the word spiritual healer is really a misnomer since it implies that the healer is capable of healing the spirit – which I'm not. I am aware that I work through and with the spirit, but the implications of this title are either very off-putting to people or, more importantly, suggestive to others that I can personally relieve their suffering, which I can't. However much I explain to people that I am merely a channel of the healing energy they receive, I am still somehow perceived as the power behind it. This belief causes a dependence on the healer, which is quite contrary to our purpose. Many healers are aware of their role as a kind of catalyst for those who seem to be guided to them with a physical problem, when their real need is so often a spiritual one. Healing seems to give people the permission they seek to awaken to the depths of their own being, whilst providing them with a sacred space in which to explore it. As our thoughts diminish and our egos hush to the rising veil, we meet our true self – maybe for the very first time. This truly is – *spiritual healing*.

As I've said before, most people seek spiritual healing for the first time as a last resort– which doesn't do much for the ego! Before seeing a new client, I first satisfy myself that they have sought medical advice. Sadly though, doctors are slow to acknowledge the deficiencies of their own role in providing complete healing. Unless we recognize the interdependence and need for balance between the physical, mental and spiritual make-up of man, however much we invest in medical research – we will never truly comprehend the nature of the disease process. Impressive though our scientific advances are, what we currently understand about disease is but a fraction of the complete picture. Never before has the Western world been so challenged by the effects of its own advancement. The increasing longevity of its population, now stretching health resources to its limits, is perhaps the time for us to wake up and discover our real needs and, indeed, the freely available resources to meet them.

PART THREE

I stroll in my garden and hear the excited chatter of the blue tits as they labour determinedly, making their nests for this year's chicks. My eyes are watchful of new green shoots breaking their way through the decay and debris of last year's growth, itself now gifting protection and sustenance to new birth. As the gentle warmth of the sun's energy falls on my back, the entirety of my being knows that winter retreats slowly into her long slumber, whilst spring emerges with new vitality and curious optimism.

How many of us are sensitive to the energies of the seasons as they come and go, some so affected by the darkened days of winter as to make them want to sleep through until spring themselves. My poor mother was one of those unfortunate people. Her dread of the oncoming January days became our dread too as we anticipated the effects of her own suffering on the rest of us. I am so fortunate to enjoy the qualities and challenges of all the seasons as they enter and leave each year but as I greet each one, I have become somewhat intrigued and yet in awe, as I recognize their reflection in the *seasons of our life*.

In a couple of months or so, starting on a specific day, *all* of France will be inconvenienced by roadworks! It doesn't matter how quickly you need to get anywhere. Your journey will be the same all the way through, whilst the queues of traffic await a man clutching a tin of white paint or, maybe, a man with a bucket of tar. There will be so many lorries lined up looking industrious but more frequently it seems – not doing very much except holding up the traffic. This will hopefully be my last experience of '*pothole repairers*' in France, but it prompts me with yet another thought on which to linger.

I don't know anything about road repairs let alone their construction. In my naivety perhaps, it would seem that the need to repair the same potholes every year suggests that the method used is ineffective and needs revising? Every winter the sub-zero temperatures crack the road surfaces and *open up old wounds*. As France's roadwork teams come out in force, they labour to patch the road so that we might journey on. How much we can learn about ourselves by just sitting patiently awaiting the *red light* to change to *green*! I am reminded of our own need for healing after exposure to the harsher elements in the winter of our lives. How very temporary that healing often seems to be, before the cracks begin to destabilize us once more. How fragile we become to our external environment, never seemingly acclimatizing to its ever-changing nature.

When we review something, we are also evaluating and hopefully learning in the process, but unless we employ the wisdom we have gained, our review is but a jigsaw – still in pieces in its box. No single part of the jigsaw is meaningful in any way until we find its adjacent partner; even then, it must grow progressively until we have the complete picture we are creating. As we diligently search for more pieces, several smaller but complete pictures emerge before finally revealing their relationship in the perfect image we have worked so attentively to attain.

I can stand back from my life now, but whilst hopefully not yet complete, I am able to see the significance of the jigsaw pieces as they sit comfortably in the bigger picture. My most intriguing observations, however, are those of my repeated attempts to try and force pieces together in disbelief of their non-compliance. How much energy and precious life over the years could perhaps have been employed more positively? How much suffering and pain could have been avoided? But I must remember – the place where I find myself now has risen through the pain, the suffering and my insistence to push all the boundaries against my own internal voice. I must remember, I had the free will to make my choices, but only now can I reflect on the purpose of those I called 'mistakes'.

Those of us who seek so earnestly to gain a clearer understanding of ourselves could perhaps be excused for coveting the spontaneous awakening of the privileged few. We question why it is so difficult for us and yet so easy for others, but in truth, none of us can appreciate the journey of another. For many people, it isn't until moving forward from this dimension to the next when their eyes have been finally opened to the reality of their own spirit. Even those of us who are in harmony with the ebb and flow of life can never fully anticipate the truth beyond our physical state. Anyone who works with very sick people for any length of time is bound to be confronted with phenomena and experiences – beyond our understanding. I have had my fair share of ghosts and 'feelings' that are bound to emerge around hospitals and such places. I have yet to go to a hospital that hasn't got its own resident ethereal nurse, doctor, patient or whoever walking the corridors at night; some of whom I *have* had the pleasure of meeting! However used to such stories (or experiences) one becomes, there is always another that takes you by surprise.

Even to this day I'm left wondering why I was on duty when a man walked down the ward to speak to me. It was a children's ward, so at first I wondered quite what he was doing there until he told me his story… as though he knew I would understand. Jack had evidently been on one of the adult wards some months previous to have a fairly routine operation. But it turned out to be far from routine when his heart stopped during surgery and he'd effectively died, before being brought back to life again. Jack had never told anyone else about his 'out of body experience' when he was aware of everything that was happening during his resuscitation (and more), even though he was clinically dead. How did this man know there was a nursing sister on the children's ward who would be able to help him? He didn't need help to understand what had happened, he just wanted to share his immense emotions with someone who would listen and hopefully also understand. He told me he would never fear death ever again and that now, with his fear dismantled, he knew how to enjoy life, as it took on a very new meaning.

I have never feared death or dying but I vividly recall as a child fearing the death of my parents. This doesn't seem to be an unusual emotion of young children, when the lights are turned out and they lie in their beds in the darkened room, their minds no longer distracted by other things. I don't know why I had these pangs of fear that seemed almost to accompany me on my arrival to this life. The sense of anxiety that loomed over so much of my childhood, when I would worry about the welfare and happiness of those close to me, always believing I could make things better, seems quite extraordinary now. I am perhaps being naïve in believing it to be a childhood trait since, whilst it may be a product of my childhood, it is a burden that has been carried far too long and been the most difficult to shed, let alone understand. But we must understand our fears if we really want to move on because that understanding is the prerequisite to self-knowledge, which alone is the only requirement for a harmonious relationship – with ourselves.

Whilst I am prompted to write these words I am reminded of their significance, not only to me but to those who read them – to most of us whose constant fear prevents us from living our true purpose. Such acknowledgement stirs discomfort within us as we try to deny its truth, but we must learn that fear is the basis of all man's problems, although the nature of its source – cleverly disguises its own identity. It's not difficult to identify an anxious child but to understand their fear...

When I was quite young, I remember very clearly just *knowing* – knowing what? I can't really put it into words but it was as though I still had another family around me – almost like a huge security blanket. It was a security blanket; I know that now. It was the protective loving energy that I came with but bit by bit, my 'other family' seemed to ebb away and with it, so did the clarity of vision I came with. My fear emerged from my feelings of separation, isolation and perhaps even rejection. I was on my own, or so I thought. I understand my feelings at the time to resemble the emotions of bereavement and loss, and as we all know, the healing process is one that can't be rushed. I have often wondered quite when the placidity of my personality (that excused my mother's forgetfulness when she left me outside the fish shop) was exchanged for one of anxiousness. But now I understand. My family (dysfunctional though it was) was loving and giving and I adored them all, but I remained feeling as though I was looking on, almost as if there was something missing. How many others have experienced these feelings I wonder?

The word *fear* is strong language representing an equally strong emotion. The word conjures up quite different scenarios for us all, ranging from the trembling knees and thumping heart when we fly in an aircraft to the sight of a spider in our bedroom. Some of us may be drawn to the shopkeeper held at knifepoint or people escaping a sinking ship; it's all an experience of fear. But I'm not speaking about the short-lived experiences of such strong emotions which are all part of our fright, flight mechanism. I'm referring to the long-term fear that dwells in us and around us for much of our lives until we confront it and dissolve it. Unfortunately, more often than not, we are unaware that we literally *live in fear* because we are so ready to blame situations, other people, and the 'hand' that life has dealt us, when we are unhappy or things go wrong for us. Fear is about as far removed from our innate nature as an angel going to war, which is why it feels so uncomfortable. When we live fearfully, we are effectively closing ourselves off from our own spiritual source by enshrouding ourselves in everything that is *not* who we are. Most of us don't hide behind the curtain all the time, allowing ourselves to meet daylight when the 'crisis' of the moment has passed.

We in the Western world have become so much the dwelling place of fear that when it leaves us for a while we are almost bereft, whilst we ask the question – *why*? I have been in that place. After living a life (I now realize) in constant fear, my enforced separation from all that was causing it was like losing a vital part of me. I can remember trying desperately to recall quite what was missing and, almost in disbelief of the place I'd once been, trying to replicate the fearful anxieties that had lived with me for so long. It sounds a strange thing to suggest that I wanted that part of me back because I certainly didn't but I became preoccupied trying to discover the reason for its disappearance. I recall that relatively short period of my life, believing I would never worry or be fearful again. It's always so simple to understand when things are going smoothly, whilst we are cocooned in a duvet of positive energy. Sometimes, if we are strong enough and determined enough to apply that knowledge when we are left in the cold again, we can truly say – 'I have learnt – I have remembered.' But most of us find that a difficult lesson to learn and as I have already acknowledged: when things get tough – we run to that with which we feel most familiar.

The nature of fear was something that I hadn't really examined, for fear of displacing my own comfort zone. The word itself is so suggestive of failure or perhaps even cowardliness, that it's not surprising we are hesitant to admit to its stronghold. And of course – it is a *hold* that we are referring to here. The reemergence of my own state of worrying after the death of my husband prompted the drive to an enquiry that has been ongoing ever since. Fear may never disappear completely from our minds but when we allow our hearts to reach out to it, we discover from whence it came – not of our *spirit* but of *our mind.*

In case you are tempted to pass by the next pages in the belief that fear has kindly passed you by – please stay a little longer; you may be grateful to have had the opportunity! If we take time to examine our own lives we will not only see how fear dominates it but how it influences our interactions and relationships with everybody around us. It becomes the foundation of our opinions and judgments, having both near and far-reaching consequences. As parents, we constantly fear that our children will not achieve at school, thus preventing them from getting a 'good job'. Our anxiety is transferred to our children. So now they too know how to fear! Even if they are doing well at school, or not even attending school yet, we can fear the latest strain of influenza every time they sneeze or get a cold. What if they contract meningitis or succumb to some other terrible fate? It's not necessary for us to have children to enable us to worry; we know that people are being made redundant in our place of work. The fear that we will be next becomes so overwhelming as to sometimes destroy our lives, by which time – we have reached retirement and escaped redundancy anyway. We sit on the train to go to work but the train is delayed. Already fearing we could be late, we read our newspaper; the banks are failing; our investments are depreciating; another young schoolboy stabbed; and just look what's happening in America... China... France! We get off the train and head for work, still anxious that we'll be late. When we get to work we have meetings to go to and deadlines to meet. Most of us accept this kind of stress as being part of our working life but actually, stress is composed of fear, not work demands. When we enter the workplace the all engaging fears we had are exchanged for other fears and by the time we arrive home – we are thankfully just in time to get an up to the minute update from the BBC newsreader!

My work as counsellor and healer has shown me over the years how many of us are acceptant of the role of fear in our lives. Sadly, it usually takes more than our acceptance to turn things around. I hear so many times how much a person wants to change things and have a more rewarding and fruitful life, but that desire alone remains an empty and unfulfilled wish until we take the first steps to releasing the chains that bind us. All the while we allow doubts to deter us, we are kept in the stronghold of that which feeds those doubts – *our minds*.

When someone asks me how they can rid themselves of fear and worry, I can only offer the same words that were given to me – *Let Go*. Our minds are so consumed with wanting to control, not just ourselves but everything and everybody around us, that we mistakenly believe we *are* our thoughts and our minds. Our need to control is initiated by our addictive and compulsive fear that arises whenever things are not acting out as *we think* they should or would like them to be. So fear only arises when we can't control something that we would prefer to. We have no control over the world economy and its effects on our purse. We have no control over our children's exam results or if they choose to take a different path to the one we were sculpting for them. We have no control if we don't come home tonight and end up in hospital instead. We have no control if we get cancer. We have no control when and how – we will die. We can take adequate precautions to safeguard ourselves and our families; we can pass our wisdom on to our young people in the hopes that they may use it, but beyond that – we must Let Go, because when we do, we also let go of our suffering that emerges from our constant need to be in control and its precursor – *fear*.

We owe it to ourselves to liberate ourselves from our ever controlling ego, which itself is in constant fear of being demoted, if not demolished altogether. If we choose to acknowledge this delusion of grandeur as being our own truth, we must also accept the suffering that will inevitably accompany that choice and so substantiate that belief. Our fear doesn't just stay with *us* – it has far-reaching consequences. It is not part of our *divine* self, but it is a very powerful energy which readily infests all those who unsuspectingly invite its negativity. We have all experienced the power of negative energy, not only in the way it affects us personally but in its ability to permeate through families, workplaces, communities and countries. One single fear-driven mind within a family or community has the potential to be more infectious than the common cold, but unlike the common cold – we are completely in control of our own immunity against it.

We must first remind ourselves that the news we hear on the television or read in the paper; the gathering of the 'professional discontents' that try to suck us in at work; the worry we feel when we can't pay the bills – are all energies of *fear*. As soon as you take any one of them on board, you will automatically attract more – and more – and more. Once we enter the door of negativism and fear, we walk away from the beauty and power of our own essence. The only way we know how to deal with our immense suffering is to paste over the current fear by replacing it with – yes – more fear. We even seek out people who are as addicted to negative thinking as ourselves, the effect being one of 'support' – or so we think.

Although most of us wouldn't agree (until we have practised), it's easy to resist the giant vacuum of negative fear by transmuting its energy to something completely positive. If you don't believe me, try it now. Don't be frightened of the strength it exerts on you, just embrace it. Get to know it and above all – love it – with all your heart. You know now that fear is just the rampant, unorganized energy of your own mind – *your thoughts*. When we have a spoilt, unruly child, we need to change his behaviour by retraining him and showing him how to utilize his energies more fruitfully, whilst at the same time lovingly reminding him that although a very special part of the family – he is *not* in control of the family. Our love overwhelms the child and his need to dominate his environment in order to be noticed, and he begins to understand his own role within the family unit. Now that he knows he is not responsible for his family a great burden is lifted from him and he can just relax, knowing exactly what is required of him. When we retrain our own mind and free it from its self-appointed responsibilities and fight for dominance, its creativity emerges from its beautiful, harmonious accord with our own *divine essence*.

My own journey through fear is far from complete, but my ongoing enquiry and the answers revealed have transported me beyond the fallacy of its encumbrance. I come across so many people who are more comfortable living in their bubble of fear than stepping beyond it and discovering what they are missing. Our minds are in such a constant state of self-preservation that anything outside our bubble becomes our enemy – to fear. My illusionary enemy at the moment is my computer! I have convinced myself that it can steal my identity or other information and, more importantly, it may carry my documents into cyberspace – which I imagine is an alien planet somewhere. Fortunately, I know the source of these ridiculous fears as being no more than my lack of knowledge, but the same key that opens that door for me is the one that can open the door for us all to – *World Peace*.

The world has entered an era of great change on all levels. There are few of us who are, or will be, unaffected by these changes in some way or another. Every part of the planet seems to be in upheaval with profound environmental extremes affecting those on many continents. All this occurs at a time of world economic crisis, which alone has caused chaos and hardship to millions, and then we hear of revolts and uprisings spreading across the Middle East, stirring pangs of unease for those of us watching from the comfort of our armchair. It's not for me to even have an opinion about the weather conditions. It's not for me to pass judgment on the economic crisis. It is, however, for all of us to perceive the relationship between our own minds and its unfounded fears that leads to hatred of – a completely illusory enemy. Before we judge a person, culture or religion from the narrow perspective of our protective bubble, we must be brave. Brave enough to step out and face our fears, embrace our *'enemies'* and discover in the process – not the destructive power of fear but the creative power of its polar opposite – Love.

When I first started to reflect on my life, it became an opportunity not only to reflect, but to review. But the cathartic exercise that has caused a major shift in my own consciousness lifts me from a place of uncertainty to a place of great optimism and hope, not just for me personally or my nearest and dearest, but for the entirety of mankind – my own brethren. It was not my original intention to share the private and somewhat sacred process of my long and often painful journey, but the urgency with which my fingers touch the keys reflects that which I know is my own purpose.

As I stroll in the stillness of the woods, my eyes catching sight of a rabbit's tail as it scampers from my path, I am reminded of the aliveness embedded even within the roots of the silent trees, as they wave knowingly in the breeze. As I try to glimpse 'Cotton Tail's' skilful descent into the undergrowth, I ponder on his oblivion of his own vulnerability caused by the limitations of his perspective on the 'ground floor' that is his world. Glancing up, I notice the squirrel, blessed with an agile swiftness that allows her the advantage to experience the vista from the great heights of any tree, that would be the envy of my 'friends' down here with me. But still way beyond the trees, winging high into the blueness of the sunlit sky, majestically soars a Kite, his keen eye scanning the whole world around and beneath him – for this morning's breakfast. I am in wonderment as I perceive his fearless presence, thus earned when his ancestors in their wisdom... first took to the wing and widened their view. I am in wonderment too of my own ever-changing truth, whilst watching it reveal itself... through my ever-changing *field of vision*.

BOOKS

O is a symbol of the world, of oneness and unity. In different cultures it also means the "eye," symbolizing knowledge and insight. We aim to publish books that are accessible, constructive and that challenge accepted opinion, both that of academia and the "moral majority."

Our books are available in all good English language bookstores worldwide. If you don't see the book on the shelves ask the bookstore to order it for you, quoting the ISBN number and title. Alternatively you can order online (all major online retail sites carry our titles) or contact the distributor in the relevant country, listed on the copyright page.

See our website **www.o-books.net** for a full list of over 500 titles, growing by 100 a year.

And tune in to myspiritradio.com for our book review radio show, hosted by June-Elleni Laine, where you can listen to the authors discussing their books.

MySpiritRadio